The Story of the Cabinet Office

LIBRARY OF POLITICAL STUDIES

GENERAL EDITOR:
PROFESSOR H. VICTOR WISEMAN
Department of Government
University of Exeter

The Story of the Cabinet Office

by R. K. Mosley

LONDON
ROUTLEDGE & KEGAN PAUL
NEW YORK: HUMANITIES PRESS

First published 1969
by Routledge & Kegan Paul Ltd
Broadway House, 68-74 Carter Lane
London, E.C.4

Printed in Great Britain
by Northumberland Press Limited,
Gateshead

SBN 7100 6600 7

General Editor's Introduction

This series of monographs is designed primarily to meet the needs of students of government, politics, or political science in Universities and other institutions providing courses leading to degrees. Each volume aims to provide a brief general introduction indicating the significance of its topic, e.g. executives, parties, pressure groups, etc., and then a longer 'case study' relevant to the general topic. First year students will thus be introduced to the kind of detailed work on which all generalizations must be based, while more mature students will have an opportunity to become acquainted with recent original research in a variety of fields. This series will eventually provide a comprehensive coverage of most aspects of political science in a more interesting and fundamental manner than in the large volume which often fails to compensate by breadth what it inevitably lacks in depth.

The present volume attempts to fill a gap in the writings about the machinery of government. Relatively little is known about the Cabinet Office despite its great significance administratively and politically. Mr Mosley has examined all the available material and traces the origin and development of the Office from before World War I to the present day. Inevitably, because of the thirty-year rule, he is better able to document his study before than after 1938. In addition to examining the personnel, method of work, and general duties of the Office, however, he has been able to use recently released material to present three 'case-studies' of actual Cabinet decisions as seen through the eyes of the Secretariat. This is, then, something of a pioneer work which should interest not only students but also participants, both political and official, in the political process.

H.W.W.

Contents

Acknowledgements

The author wishes to express his thanks to the following:

1 The staff at the Public Record Office, London W.C.2. for their friendly and efficient service at all times.
2 Mr J. Ashton and Mrs P. Robertson at the Commonwealth Secretariat for their helpful answers to his enquiries.
3 The following publishers for permission to quote from their works:
   (a) Allen & Unwin, Hankey, *The Supreme Command*, 1961,
   (b) Benn Bros., Hankey, *Diplomacy by Conference*, 1946,
   (c) Cassell & Co., Churchill, *The Second World War*,
   (d) The Rt. Hon. Harold Wilson and B.B.C. Publications Ltd, *The Listener*, 6 April 1967.
4 The Controller of H.M. Stationery Office for permission to reproduce extracts from the following Crown-copyright records in the Public Record Office:
   (a) Cabinet Minutes, reference CAB 23-48; CAB 23-67; CAB 23-68.
   (b) P.R.O. Handbook—Records of the Cabinet Office to 1922.

1
How it began

The Victorian era was a time of more exciting political
changes than any other period in British history. Cabinets
met and made momentous decisions covering the whole
gamut of political activities. New empires were built,
alliances formed and battles fought; social legislation was
passed on an unprecedented scale; extended franchises
and railways led to political parties being organized on a
national basis as never before; a pattern of elected local
councils developed to cover the whole face of England
and Wales—all this and more was directed by Her
Majesty's ministers without a committee clerk to call
their own, an agenda paper to keep them in order or
written minutes to record their decisions. Even the Pick-
wick Club kept its records, but not so the British Cabinet.
This surely must be one of the most remarkable non-
happenings since the invention of pen and ink.

It would not be correct to think that Cabinet minutes
had never been kept. In the first place the Cabinet is a
direct descendant of the Privy Council and records exist
of Council meetings held as far back as the fourteenth

century. Dicey, in 'The Privy Council', gives this charming example from those early records: 'And these words and many other gentle words he said benignly and goodly, that tears sprung as well out of his eyes as out of the eyes of all my said Lords that were there present.' (Hankey, 1946, 42)

Secondly, the Cabinet had been firmly established by the time of George III and George IV, during whose reigns standardized minutes were certainly kept. Hankey quotes another instance of a 'Minute of Cabinet', written at a Cabinet meeting held on 27 November 1779: 'Agreed to recommend to his Majesty to raise as soon as possible eight thousand men in Ireland to be employed wherever His Majesty shall please to direct.' Hankey drily adds 'That strikes me as an admirable minute.' (Hankey, 1946, 49)

Such records of Cabinet meetings as were made during the eighteenth and nineteenth centuries, however, do seem to cease after the accession of Queen Victoria. Possibly the explanation is that by then the Cabinet was no longer an advisory council of ministers seeking approval of the Sovereign for its recommendations. It was more an executive committee of Parliament, or to use Bagehot's famous phrase, 'a hyphen which joins, a buckle which fastens the legislative part of the state to the executive part'. Consequently there was no need to submit proposals in the form of minutes for Royal confirmation.

Furthermore, following the 1832 Reform Act, ministers gradually recognized the need for close links between their thinking and that of the majority party in the Commons, whose members' allegiance could no longer be bought by patronage or bribery. M.P.s depended on the electorate for their position. Hence developed the principle of collective responsibility, that Cabinet members must support each other on all major issues, since ministerial disunity might herald political disaster. It might have been felt that the image of solidarity would be more difficult to project if it were recorded, however confidentially, that on some measures members were at variance with one another. Also an understandable fear of Cabinet leakages, albeit of issues on which there was full agreement, almost certainly influenced the ministers. When, nearly one hundred years later, it was decided to minute Cabinet proceedings systematically many M.P.s objected, one declaring, 'You will need almost an Army Corps to protect the secrecy of these records.'

Whatever the reasons, throughout the reign of Queen Victoria, no official Cabinet records were made apart from the report to the Queen, personally written by the Prime Minister of the day. Incidentally, it is plain from the Queen's own correspondence that different Prime Ministers held different views as to how much should be divulged to Her Majesty concerning minority opinions within the Cabinet. Some, like Lord Melbourne, would give Her Majesty detailed accounts of disagreements at Cabinet meetings, mentioning names quite freely. By contrast, Mr Gladstone was quite specific that the Queen ought not to be told about clashes of opinion within the Cabinet; an attitude which, not surprisingly, incurred the Royal displeasure. The Cabinet's conclusions (i.e. minutes) of today support Gladstone's view since names of dissentients from the general will are not normally noted.

The Committee of Imperial Defence

It is generally known that the Cabinet Secretariat was established officially by Lloyd George in 1916. But there is a direct link between this Secretariat and that of the Committee of Imperial Defence and therefore something should be said of how this latter organization came into being.

Perhaps a starting point could be the establishment in 1881 of a Royal Commission 'on the defence of British Possessions and Commerce Abroad', even though this august sounding body did little more than consider plans for the defence of navy coaling stations. (Ehrmann, 1958, 9) The Commission did at least have a secretary who served also as secretary to a new Colonial Defence Committee set up in 1885. The original secretary of this Defence Committee was soon succeeded by Lord Sydenham of Coombe. His staff comprised one clerk and one typist, yet during the next twenty years Lord Sydenham's quiet influence in defence discussions was of considerable value and it was fitting that he should eventually become the first secretary to the Committee of Imperial Defence.

This last Committee arose, at least in part, from the general misgivings which had been felt over the administrative shortcomings displayed by the Army in its conduct of the Boer War at the turn of the century. An investigating commission under Lord Elgin blamed the Cabinet rather than the War Office for many of these deficiencies. To his credit Balfour, the new Conservative Prime Minister, acted swiftly and in December 1902 he established a Committee of Imperial Defence whose function was to advise the Cabinet on strategic planning for military purposes, on co-ordinating Navy and Army aims and activities and on measures needed to ensure that the Services were in a constant state of readiness for any operational purpose.

From the start, Balfour was determined to have both Cabinet members and Service chiefs on the C.I.D. This was one reason why he had decided that it was not enough to reconstitute the Defence Committee of the Cabinet. A further reason was that it would now be possible to ignore the conventional secrecy of Cabinet meetings and instead keep proper records of proceedings which could be both detailed and informative. To quote from Balfour's speech in the House of Commons when members were debating the setting up of the C.I.D.:

The Committee will keep records and the records will not consist of bare resolutions saying so many men are required for this or that purpose, so many ships are necessary for this or that need. We shall have something much more than that, namely the full-blooded and detailed account of the reasons on which the conclusions come to be based. (H.C. Debates, 5 March 1903)

The Prime Minister in fact regarded this matter of 'conclusions' as the most important reason of all for the C.I.D., emphasizing that it was 'the first great difference' between previous Cabinet Defence committees and his new Committee.

If so much emphasis was to be given to the recording of discussions and decisions, clearly there had to be proper machinery available. This was eventually established by what was to become an historic Treasury Minute of 4 May 1904, which recognized the creation of a Secretariat for the Committee of Imperial Defence by making available funds to maintain a permanent staff. The staff in fact comprised one secretary, two assistant secretaries, an army officer and a naval officer, and about six clerks. Such were the beginnings of the modern Cabinet Office, Mr Wilson's 'powerhouse' with five hundred personnel and an annual budget of one million pounds. This Treasury Minute of 1904 described the Secretariat's responsibilities to be: 'the preservation of the records of the C.I.D.'s deliberations; the procurement of information and documents on Imperial Defence for the C.I.D.; the provision of continuity of method in the treatment of questions which may come before the C.I.D.' This last duty was especially significant. Prime Ministers may differ in their knowledge of and enthusiasm for defence issues. But at least if there is an efficient Secretariat the dangers of such inconsistency are minimized since any problems, in this case of Imperial Defence, are systematically brought to the notice of the Prime Minister who can be assisted in dealing with them by an accurate informative resumé of relevant previous discussions and proposals.

New creations are often suspect and the Secretariat of the C.I.D. was no exception. However much Balfour personally might protest that the functions of the Committee itself were only advisory, it was unfortunately true that among supporters of the C.I.D. concept were those such as Lord Esher who advocated a strong Secretariat with power of initiative to 'anticipate' the needs of both the Prime Minister and the C.I.D. The mere fact that the Secretariat was clearly to be the Premier's own 'general staff' gave it status. Fisher, the zealous First Sea Lord, was always suspicious of any proposal which he felt might weaken his own power with the Navy. He was largely responsible for the dismissal in 1907 of Lord Sydenham, the C.I.D.'s Secretary, because, Fisher alleged, Sydenham had sought to persuade the Prime Minister to resist the Navy's plan for the construction of Dreadnoughts. Sydenham was succeeded by Captain Charles Ottley, who remained as Secretary until May 1912, when he was replaced by the legendary Maurice Hankey who had been appointed Ottley's assistant in 1908. Hankey had been recommended by Fisher to the War Secretary in the following terms: 'There is a captain of Marines called Hankey, serving in the Mediterranean Fleet. He has a large forehead bulging with brains. He has been created by God Almighty for the express discomfiture of Kaiser Wilhelm II. Get him to the C.I.D. as soon as you can.' (Ismay, 1960, 43) A useful testimonial.

During the following years general misgivings about the Committee of Imperial Defence were partly assuaged. Campbell Bannerman for instance, an early doubter, was later to describe it as 'an invaluable addition to Britain's constitutional machinery'. (Johnson, 1960, 82) Meanwhile, the Secretariat quietly pursued its own task of easing the administrative burdens which beset the C.I.D. The growing danger of war with Germany meant that careful preparations had to be made in anticipation of *'Der Tag'*. To this end the Secretariat was largely responsible for compiling the famous War Book, which systematically listed all the foreseeable steps to be taken should war come and named the Government departments responsible for taking these measures as and when the time arose. According to Lord Oxford, 'Inquiries were inaugurated into such matters as the treatment of enemy and neutral shipping; enemy trade; our own supplies; control of railways and ports; insurance of ships and cargoes against war risks; counter-espionage; censorship; treatment of enemy aliens; cable and wireless communications.' (Hankey, 1946, 89) Between 1909 and 1914 these and other relevant issues were methodically examined by a series of sub-committees, the conclusions, after approval by the Committee of Imperial Defence, being embodied in the War Book. There was no shortage of work here for the liveliest of secretariats, delving as they did even into such detail as the timing of troop trains.

Today, with our experience of two world wars and knowledge of the vast amount of organization they entailed—conscription of men and women, material and property; rationing of food and petrol; commandeering of private property for military purposes; etc.—it is difficult for us to realize how startling such issues must have been to those Edwardians planning for the contingency of total war. Every other war in British history had been fought by a handful of professional soldiers. A hundred years of relative peace did not help the C.I.D. in its efforts to convince all concerned of the immediacy of the danger. Everything considered, Hankey may be forgiven his modest observation that their defensive arrangements 'were not ineffective'.

As war became imminent, the pressure upon the Secretariat's members increased, but they proved more than adequate in handling the deluge of administrative minutiae showered upon them.

Special arrangements had been made so that in every office responsible officials should be ready at all hours to take immediate action. The requisite telegrams—amounting to thousands—were carefully arranged in order of priority of despatch so as to prevent congestion on the day of action; every possible letter and document was kept ready in an addressed envelope; special envelopes were designed so that they could at once be recognized as taking priority of everything. All necessary papers, Orders in Council and Proclamations were printed or set up in type, and so far was the system carried that the King never moved without having with him those which required his immediate signature. (Hankey, 1946, 91)

Efficient secretariats might not make the headlines but there can be little doubting their worth.

The 1914-18 War

The administrative adjustments made to the Cabinet machinery during the first two years of war are beyond the scope of this book. But it may help to tabulate the major changes which affected Hankey's men. These were:

1914 A War Council was established, taking over from the C.I.D. the latter's responsibility for general policy. (After all, the C.I.D. was only advisory, and something much more forceful was now required.)

1915 The War Council was replaced by the Dardanelles Committee which, despite its name, soon became a War Committee of the Cabinet.

1916   Lloyd George, on becoming Prime Minister, abolished the War Committee and established a War Cabinet of five ministers, of whom only the Chancellor of the Exchequer held departmental responsibilities.

For our purposes the significant things about these administrative experiments was that in each case the Secretariat taken over from the C.I.D. served the new organization. Thus a vital element of continuity was maintained which preserved some order at the highest level throughout those anxious years.

Many varied accounts of how Asquith was supplanted by Lloyd George as Prime Minister have been written. (One as reliable and certainly as readable as any is in Roy Jenkins' brilliant biography, *Asquith*.) But what concerns us here is not how the member for Caernarvon Boroughs became Prime Minister but the changes he made within hours of taking office. Putting first things first, he stopped the practice of having an advisory committee which varied in composition and number from meeting to meeting. ('Trying to run the war with a Sanhedrin' was a typical Lloyd Georgian phrase). Instead, he established a War Cabinet of four non-departmental ministers (Lloyd George, Curzon, Milner and Henderson) plus Bonar Law, the Chancellor of the Exchequer. Simultaneously he promoted Hankey and his staff to be responsible for all the secretarial assistance which his new Cabinet required. On 11 December 1916, Hankey began to draft his Rules of Procedure. After two hundred years gestation, the Cabinet Secretariat was born, charged with the following responsibilities:

1. To record the proceedings of the War Cabinet.

2. To transmit the decisions of the War Cabinet to those departments which are concerned in giving effect to them or otherwise interested.

3. To prepare the agenda papers; to arrange for the attendance of ministers and other persons concerned; and to procure and circulate the documents required for discussion.

4. To attend to the correspondence connected with the work of the War Cabinet.

2

The years of consolidation

The Scope and Size of the Job

Production of paper-work and the holding of meetings are by themselves no indication of the working efficiency of any organization. But it is worthwhile recording the following data of meetings serviced by the Cabinet Secretariat, given by Lord Curzon in the House of Lords on 19 June 1918: 'Between 9th December 1916 and 3rd May 1917, the Cabinet met 146 times in 125 days excluding Sundays. From 20th September 1917 to 12th February 1918 there were 131 meetings in 125 working days.' During 1917-19 over 500 outsiders were summoned to attend Cabinet meetings by the Secretariat (H.M.S.O., 1966, 3), which also had to service 92 Cabinet committees within the same period (H.M.S.O., 1966, 15).

Apart from their direct responsibilities to the Cabinet, the Secretariat had also during these years to perform similar duties for the Imperial War Cabinet (meetings of leading Dominion statesmen), the British Section of the Supreme War Cabinet and in 1919, the British Empire Delegation during the Peace Conference in Paris. At home, new departments were established at a pace unparalleled in our administrative history (e.g., Labour on 11 December; Shipping, Food and Pensions on 22 December 1916). In all, eleven new ministries were established before the end of the war and this involved the setting up of well over one hundred inter-departmental committees, each with its own agenda and minutes to be prepared for every meeting. The administration of these non-Cabinet institutions lies outside the purlieu of this book, but it could be fairly claimed that much was owed to the Secretariat's work behind the scenes.

The Content of the Job

What in fact did this work involve? Its extent can be illustrated by quoting from the Rules of Procedure drafted by Hankey, approved by the War Cabinet and which read as follows:

(1) *Reference.* Questions may be referred for decision by the War Cabinet by the Prime Minister, or by Members of the War Cabinet, or by any Member of the Government, or by any Government Department. The normal procedure for raising any question should be by a communication to the Secretary, accompanied, when practicable, by a short Memorandum containing a summary of the points on which a decision is required.

(2) *Consultation with Departments.* Before reaching their final conclusions on any subject the War Cabinet will, as a general rule, consult the Ministers at the head of the Departments concerned, who will lay before them all the evidence, written or oral, relevant and necessary to a decision.

(3) *Approval of Minutes.* After each meeting the Secretary will circulate copies of the draft Minutes to members for their remarks. He will also circulate to Ministers summoned for particular subjects, drafts of the Minutes on

those subjects for their remarks. When their remarks have been received, the Secretary will submit a final draft of the Minutes for the approval of the Prime Minister. After the Prime Minister has initialled the Minutes of the War Cabinet, the conclusions formulated therein will become operative decisions to be carried out by the responsible Departments. The Prime Minister can delegate his powers in this respect in case of absence or the claims of other urgent business.

(4) *Circulation of Minutes.* As soon as the Prime Minister's initials have been received, the decisions of the War Cabinet will be communicated by the Secretary to the Political and Civil Heads of the Departments concerned, who will be responsible for giving effect to them.

(5) *Communication to the War Cabinet and Certain Departments for Record.* The Secretary will also communicate complete copies of the Minutes of the War Cabinet for record to all Members of the War Cabinet, and to the following Heads of Departments, as decided by the War Cabinet: Secretaries of State for Home Affairs; Foreign Affairs; War; the Colonies; India; also to the First Lord of the Admiralty and the President of the Board of Trade.

Copies of all decisions affecting the War will also be sent for record to: First Sea Lord; Chief of the Imperial General Staff; and Under Secretary of State for Foreign Affairs.

The only exception to this rule will be in the case of decisions of extreme secrecy (such as, the dates of forthcoming operations, new engines of war, etc.), the reproduction of which is not advisable; in such cases the Prime Minister may, on the advice of the War Cabinet, use his discretion to withhold either wholly, or for a time, the communication of copies of the Minutes.

Under the instructions of the Prime Minister the Secretary may communicate particular decisions direct to Chairmen of Committees, and others whom they affect.

(6) *The Carrying out of the Decisions of the War Cabinet.*

13

In order to keep the War Cabinet fully informed, the Head of the Department responsible for action on any of the War Cabinet's decisions is requested to notify the Secretary as to the action taken, or, if for any reason action is found impossible or unnecessary, to notify him accordingly. Where applicable, it would be convenient if the communication to the Secretary could take the form of copies or paraphrases of the telegrams, letters, or instructions, actually sent.

(7) *The Attendance of Experts.* The First Sea Lord of the Admiralty, the Chief of the Imperial Staff, and the Permanent Under-Secretary of the Foreign Office, or their representatives, will ordinarily attend at the outset of each meeting to explain respectively the latest developments of the naval, military, and political situation, and will remain as long as necessary according to the nature of the business to be transacted. Other experts may be summoned as required.

(8) *The Communication of Information by Departments.* Heads of Departments are requested to communicate to the Secretary, for the use of the War Cabinet, all information bearing on the higher conduct of the war, or on any other question concerning the War Cabinet, whether consisting of telegrams, despatches, memoranda, statistics, Reports of Committees etc. In the case of bulky documents attention should be drawn to passages bearing more particularly on current questions. (H.M.S.O., 1966, 51)

Item (4) was of some constitutional significance since the fact that Cabinet decisions were henceforth to be communicated directly to the respective departments by the Cabinet Secretary and not, as hitherto, passed down by the Cabinet Minister concerned to his Permanent Secretary; was bound to fetter a minister's discretionary powers as regards how much he chose to tell his own staff about Cabinet decisions which affected their department.

In practice Item (6) was also significant since the wisest of decisions are useless unless they are promptly executed, and this rule empowered the Secretariat to keep prodding tactfully but effectively any neglectful ministry.

But perhaps two of the most important of these tasks were the preparation of agendas and the recording of minutes or 'conclusions' as they came to be called, and it is worth looking more closely into how the Secretariat organized these duties.

The Preparation of Agendas

This work needed special care as most issues requiring a decision at each meeting of the five-member War Cabinet concerned 'outside' ministers to all of whom the doctrine of collective responsibility also applied, of course. Hankey developed considerable finesse in deciding which matters should be included in any particular agenda. Although in theory a Cabinet Minister could raise a new item at any meeting, this was seldom done. The usual practice was that when a ministry wished to put up a matter for Cabinet decision a request for its inclusion in the agenda would be sent to the Cabinet Secretary accompanied by any relevant papers. Copies of these papers and notice of the request would then be circulated by the Secretariat to enable other departments possibly concerned to comment on the item if they wished. Where feasible agendas were prepared and circulated one or two days in advance. I say, 'where feasible' because there were sometimes two or even three Cabinet meetings in one day.

Clearly, for most meetings there would be several 'outsiders' to be summoned. (Sometimes over twenty of them crowding into the Cabinet room.) Clearly too, there was always a danger that some issue might involve a department which the Secretariat had overlooked. Hankey's method of dealing with these two separate points provide a good example of his thoroughness.

First, each item would have a tentative time-table appended to it in order to give those summoned an approximate idea as to when their presence would be needed. Secondly, the names of those non-Cabinet ministers and others required to attend would be noted on the back of the agenda paper with a reference to the specific item with which they were concerned. Thirdly, the agendas were normally sent out to all major departments thus giving each the chance to see if it had been accidentally excluded or, conversely, if it had been wrongly included to discuss a topic in which it was not (any longer) involved. Fourthly, ministers would be issued each Monday with a list of outstanding topics, i.e. those which had been already raised by a ministry but which were either still in the queue waiting to be placed on the agenda, or still pending as a result of the Cabinet's failure to reach a decision. Fifthly, a Distribution List was kept which referenced all departmental papers received for Cabinet discussion and items on the List would be deleted when they had been dealt with by the Cabinet. It was from the undeleted items on the Distribution List that agendas were drafted, for it provided a useful summary of outstanding business together with the relevant papers and departments involved. Last, whilst the Cabinet meeting was actually in progress, Hankey would judge when his clerks outside should send warning messages to the visitors needed for the next item's discussion. (Sometimes, of course, the message would be to delay their arrival, since discussion on preceding items was running behind schedule.) By this means, the non-productive waiting time of all concerned was reduced to a minimum. Cabinet office efficiency was truly based on a capacity for taking pains.

The first item on each Agenda was usually 'Statements', i.e. the latest reports of the war on land and sea, given by the Chief of Imperial General Staff and the First Sea

Lord, or their deputies. The military and naval experts would then withdraw unless some general issue of war strategy was to be discussed. The next item was often a brief review of the latest foreign and diplomatic developments attended by the Foreign Secretary. After this, the agenda items would relate to those issues brought up for decision by a department or committee. Even with a small Cabinet, it soon became impossible for meetings to end with all items concluded. After a while, Hankey found it expedient to keep a register of unfinished business and 'insisted' that half an hour should be allowed at the start of each meeting to clear up these outstanding issues. (Daalder, 1964, 245)

Distribution of Minutes

The procedure for circulating 'conclusions' of the Cabinet was equally thorough. The Secretary would be present throughout the meeting but two or more Assistant Secretaries would also attend in turn, recording the proceedings in perhaps one-hour shifts. A meeting might begin at 11.30 a.m. At 12.30 p.m. the first 'recorder' would be replaced by the second. Whereupon he (No. 1) would return to his office to begin drafting then dictating his minutes. After another hour, he would return to the Cabinet Room to allow No. 2 to prepare his minutes. And so on, although, of course, in practice few Cabinet meetings lasted three hours or more.

When the meeting was over, Hankey would return to his office and check the scripts which would then be awaiting him. After approval by the Secretary, the draft minutes would be duplicated and copies sent to those who had attended the meeting (non-Cabinet attenders would receive only relevant extracts from the complete minutes). These drafts were to be checked and any inaccuracy pointed out to the Secretariat within twenty-four hours.

Finally, the conclusions, including any necessary revisions, were printed and distributed to all authorized to receive full copies, which included the King as well as those referred to in the Rules of Procedure quoted previously. The Prime Minister quickly found that he could trust the Secretariat to perform this job reliably and soon stopped asking to see the draft minutes before circulation.

The production of both agenda and conclusions for any meeting was controlled by a Duty Officer for that day's meeting and he would be responsible for all arrangements concerning the Cabinet meeting on his day of duty. These officers worked on a roster basis and would learn, usually a week ahead, when their service in this capacity was required. The job would normally include the issuing of agenda papers, informing 'outsiders' when their attendance was required, circulation and subsequent collecting of draft minutes, incorporation of any necessary revisions and the final distribution of the printed minutes, perhaps two or three days after the meeting. This work was usually carried out by an Assistant Secretary and not the least merit of the duty officer arrangement was that it gave to the participants invaluable experience of every aspect of the Secretariat's work. Below this Assistant Secretary level, staff were employed on normal office duties such as: accounts, establishment, registry, typing, distribution, indexing and filing. These last two operations involved a system devised by Hankey personally, which earned him a high reputation for an ability to produce any Cabinet minute or paper required, with remarkable speed.

War-time Criticisms of the Secretariat

When it is realized that this kind of service was being provided for sometimes as many as forty committees simultaneously, it comes almost as a shock to find that time and again the Cabinet Office was subject to attack from M.P.s and other sources. Criticisms were based mainly on three charges, viz: that unnecessary expenditure, if not downright extravagance, had been incurred by the Secretariat; that the minutes were on occasions slanted to record what Hankey felt ought to have been resolved rather than what actually was decided; and that certain members of the Secretariat, especially Hankey, far from being mere 'recorders and transmitters' were influencing the Prime Minister on decisions of Government policy, and even military strategy.

The first allegation, extravagance, seems difficult to substantiate although attempts to do so were made in a Supply debate in the Commons in March 1917. One M.P. referred to '36 gentlemen in their upholstered rooms to look after five members of this extraordinary Cabinet'. (H.C. Debates, 8 March 1917) Conditions in the Cabinet Office, at No. 2 Whitehall Gardens where once Disraeli lived and wrote his letters to Lady Chesterfield and others, were certainly more pleasant than those on the Western Front, but No. 2 was no more luxuriously furnished than were other ministries at that time. According to Hankey, the work was carried on in conditions of the greatest discomfort and over-crowding. Typists and distributing clerks worked in cellars, attics and anywhere they could.

Similarly, the second charge of inaccurate minuting seems to have little substance although anyone with much committee experience will probably agree that, with the best will in the world, inaccuracies and ambiguities may occur in the summarizing of discussions. One assistant secretary has written: 'The one injunction Hankey burned upon our souls was that a minute must always end with a definite decision. This was not easy after some particularly woolly discussions. But my experience was that if one invented the best decision one could think of, it was rarely queried by those concerned.' (Daalder, 1964, 49) Incidentally, at first, minutes included a summary of the main speeches. It was not until 1923 that the pattern was established of recording final decisions and little else.

The third criticism, that the Secretariat's senior staff sometimes influenced top-level Government decisions, is however difficult to deny. But first an important distinction must be made. As well as establishing an official Cabinet Secretariat, Lloyd George also established about the same time a separate Prime Minister's Secretariat to advise him on any matter he liked to throw at them. Its members included George Adams, Gladstone Professor of Political Theory and Political Institutions; Waldorf Astor, millionaire owner of the *Observer*; Philip Kerr, Marquess of Lothian, who had worked in South Africa under Lord Milner; David Davies, Parliamentary Secretary to Lloyd George, who had been brought back from France; and Joseph Davies, commercial statistician and author of *The Prime Minister's Secretariat*. These personal advisers of Lloyd George worked in the gardens of No. 10 Downing Street, in quickly erected huts which became known in Whitehall circles as 'the Garden Suburb'. There is no doubt that these men did influence the Premier, indeed that was their *raison d'être*. And it is understandable if outsiders failed to distinguish sharply between these two Secretariats.

For the record, the Cabinet Secretariat in its early days included the following military and civilian personnel, employed as Assistant Secretaries: Colonels Ernest Swinton and Dalby Jones; Major Storr (these three were all members of the earlier C.I.D. Secretariat); Tom Jones; Fleet-Paymaster Row and Captain Clement Jones. The practice soon developed of adding one or two M.P.s on a temporary basis, and among those to be included were Sir Mark Sykes, Colonel L. S. Amery, the Hon. W. Ormsby-Gore, and Colonel L. Wilson. Amery and Ormsby-Gore later became Cabinet Ministers, Leslie Wilson a Chief Whip for the Conservatives. All these were highly capable men but special mention should be made of Tom Jones. Hankey quickly learnt to value this remarkable Welshman 'foisted'—to use Hankey's own word—on him by Lloyd George. Tom Jones had been, amongst other things, a 9/- a week thirteen-year-old in a Welsh steelworks and a Professor of Economics at Belfast, and he was later to become Deputy Secretary to the Cabinet Office. He probably shared as many confidences with Lloyd George as did any man (they sometimes conversed in Welsh) and Jones was entrusted with several confidential missions on the Prime Minister's behalf.

To return to the charge that Hankey and others exceeded their terms of reference. Apart from the activities of the Prime Minister's 'Garden Suburb' entourage, Hankey himself was clearly much more than a recorder, as the following extracts from his diary show:

1916—December 13th:
Breakfast alone with Ll. G. at 9.15 a.m.
[This particular entry goes on] War Cabinet at 11.30, lunch in the office, dictating conclusions the while; War Cabinet at 3 p.m., dictated conclusions during the tea interval; War Cabinet at 6 p.m. Killing! (Hankey, 1961, 595)

1917—February 11th (Sunday):
Had a brainwave on the subject of anti-submarine warfare so ran down to Walton Heath in the afternoon to formulate my ideas to Ll. G. who was very interested. I sat up late completing a long memo. on the subject. (Hankey, 1961, 645)

This paper, it could be claimed, was to become one of the most important in naval history since it influenced the decision to introduce the convoy system. At that time the unrestricted submarine warfare activities of the Germans were inflicting heavy casualties on British Merchant shipping. Hankey, it must be remembered, was an ex-Marine, and for years had been Secretary to the Committee of

Imperial Defence. So it is not surprising that with his fertile mind and military experience he could and did produce many inventive ideas concerning the prosecution of the war in general, e.g., armed rollers to crush down barbed wire, bullet-proof shields and tanks. (The story is told of a proposal being sent to the War Office in 1912 for a tank 'superior in design to the tanks which fought in 1916', where the suggestion was duly pigeonholed with the file comment: 'The man's mad.') (Somervell, 1935, 121)

1918—February 15th:
As a result of our talk [Milner, Bonar Law, Wilson, Lloyd George and Hankey, after dinner at Lloyd George's London home] the Prime Minister decided that Wilson should replace Robertson as Chief of the Imperial General Staff and if Derby, the War Minister, resigned in protest against the decision, Milner should become Secretary of State for War. (Hankey, 1961, 778)

This decision caused much heart-burning. Curzon (then Lord President) and Long (Colonial Secretary), as well as Derby, considered resignation. Both Derby and Long sought Hankey's advice, as other leading statesmen also often did. Smuts, for instance, 'frequently consulted' Hankey on the proposal to amalgamate the Royal Flying Corps and the Royal Naval Air Service into one combined air force. (Hankey, 1961, 849)

Another well-substantiated instance of extra-mural activity by a Secretariat member, though slightly after the war period, was the part played by Tom Jones in persuading Michael Collins to attend an important meeting with Lloyd George at No. 10, a meeting which led to a settlement of the terrible Irish problem of the early twenties, and the eventual creation of the Irish Republic.

In Defence of the Secretariat

The use of tanks, the introduction of a convoy system,

22

the establishment of the R.A.F.—no secretary needed to be ashamed of promoting these ideas in war-time even if, in so doing, he exceeded his nominal authority. On the whole, the Cabinet Secretariat was recognized as constituting a vital part of the war machine. Lord Curzon's description of Cabinet administration in pre-Secretariat days is often quoted, but bears repetition. Speaking in the House of Lords on 19 June 1918, he said:

My noble friends will bear me out when I say that meetings of the Cabinet were most irregular, sometimes only once, seldom more than twice a week. There was no agenda, there was no order of business. Any minister requiring to bring up a matter, either of Departmental or of public importance, had to seek the permission of the Prime Minister to do so. No one else, broadly speaking, was warned in advance. It was difficult for any Minister to secure an interstice in the general discussion in which he could place his own case. No record whatever was kept of our proceedings, except the private and personal letter written by the Prime Minister to the Sovereign, the contents of which, of course, are never seen by anybody else. The Cabinet often had the very haziest notice as to what its decisions were, and I appeal not only to my own experience but to the experience of every Cabinet Minister who sits in this House, and to the records contained in the memoirs of half a dozen Prime Ministers in the past, that cases frequently arose when the matter was left so much in doubt that a Minister went away and acted upon what he thought was a decision which subsequently turned out to be no decision at all, or was repudiated by his colleagues. No one will deny that a system, however embedded in the traditions of the past and consecrated by constitutional custom, which was attended by these defects, was a system which was destined, immediately it came into contact with the hard realities of war, to crumble into dust at once.

Those in the know recognized the Secretariat's worth

and many tributes were paid by them. In the speech quoted, Lord Curzon went on to say that 'When history is written he [Hankey] will deserve his own niche in the temple which records the builders of our own national Constitution.' Years later Vansittart, a leading civil servant in the thirties, wrote of his professional colleague, 'Hankey had an incredible memory . . . which could reproduce on call the date, file and substance of every paper that ever flew into a pigeon-hole. If St Peter is as well served, there will be no errors on Judgement Day.' (Vansittart, 1958, 164) And whilst it may be an exaggeration to say of Hankey, as Balfour did, that without him we would not have won the war, Parliament granted him an armistice gift of £25,000 for his services to the Nation, and the King made him a K.C.B. Parliament also allowed his name, Lt. Col. Sir Maurice Hankey, to be included in a list of fighting Naval, Army and Air Force officers, though not without objection from some M.P.s (Beaverbrook, 1956, xix)

The Immediate Post-War Years

The cessation of hostilities was followed with almost indecent haste and against the King's wishes, by the notorious 'coupon' election of December 1918, which kept the Coalition Government in office, with Lloyd George remaining as Prime Minister. But peace brought no respite for the Secretariat. During most of 1919 Hankey and others were occupied at Versailles in the wrangling over peace terms. (One prophetic piece of drafting done there in which Hankey and Kerr had a part, was entitled 'Some Considerations for the Peace Conference before they finally draft their terms.' One section of this memorandum referred to the proposal to place two million Germans in the Polish Corridor under the Poles. The drafters expressed their fear that this would sooner or later lead to a new war in the East of Europe.)

Even during the war the concept of a small non-departmental Cabinet had had its critics. In theory, the idea was attractive but in practice it was not easy to decide which top-level inter-departmental issues were important enough to go up to the Cabinet. Despite all the Secretariat could do to minimize the work-load for their masters, the War Cabinet had found itself ruling on such issues as: Could the roof of Charterhouse School be repaired? Should meat be allowed in dog biscuits? Should pheasants be shot in March? Once the war was over priorities had to change, with social and domestic problems demanding their rightful share of attention. In consequence, the Prime Minister, in 1919, returned to the 'traditional' idea of a Cabinet which included the heads of most of the main departments. He did, however, decide to retain the Cabinet Secretariat, his other war-time innovation affecting Cabinet procedure. This latter decision, opposed by some, was supported by the famous Haldane Committee on the Machinery of Government which published its report in December 1918, (Command 9230). The Report commented, *inter alia*:

We think there is one feature in the procedure of the War Cabinet which may assume a permanent form, namely the appointment of a Secretary to the Cabinet charged with the duty of collecting and putting into shape its agenda, of providing the information and material necessary for its deliberations and of drawing records of results for communication to the departments concerned.

The permanent establishment of the Secretariat was officially authorized by the Treasury in March 1920 and its basic organization, as described in the Public Record Office publication, 'The Records of the Cabinet Office to 1922', was as follows:

There was then a division of the Office into two main branches dealing respectively with home and external affairs. The work of these departments frequently overlapped, however, and there was the closest co-ordination between them. The Secretary personally attended meetings of the Cabinet and of the Committee of Imperial Defence, as well as all international conferences. For assistance he would draw on the staff of either of the two sub-divisions of the Office, according to the nature of the business under discussion. Thus at the Washington Conference, when the agenda covered disarmament and Far Eastern questions, his assistants were from the branch which dealt with external affairs; but for the Genoa Conference, which dealt with economic matters, he chose to draw for assistance on the home affairs experts. The Home Affairs Branch, under Thomas Jones as principal assistant secretary, dealt with all domestic matters and maintained liaison with government departments concerned with home affairs. His two assistants divided these departments between them, each dealing with all communications with the departments for which he was responsible. This branch also provided the secretaries for all committees dealing with domestic matters, including the most important Home Affairs Committee. The Treasury representative seconded to the Cabinet Office in January 1920 to ensure that the financial aspects of all questions submitted to the Cabinet had been reviewed by the Treasury was also attached to the Home Affairs Branch. This officer also acted as secretary of the Finance Committee, dealt with any other matters involving finance matters, and was responsible for keeping the weekly list of subjects awaiting consideration by the Cabinet.

The branch dealing with external affairs was in 1920 known as the Imperial, Foreign and Defence Branch. By 1922 it had been renamed the Committee of Imperial Defence Branch. The three assistant secretaries or principals in this branch were seconded by the War Office, the Admiralty and the India Office. This branch was responsible for the Committee of Imperial Defence and its sub-committees, for any other Cabinet committees dealing with defence matters or external affairs, and with liaison with the relevant departments. The staff to assist the Secretary at meetings of the Supreme Council and at most international conferences would be drawn from this section. It was also responsible for circulating papers to the governments of the Dominions and of India. In November 1919 a League of Nations Branch was established under an assistant secretary seconded from the Foreign Office. All communications to and from the League of Nations were sent, for the purpose of distribution among departments concerned, to this branch of the Cabinet Office. The head of this section also accompanied the British members of the Council and Assembly of the League of Nations to all meetings of those bodies. (H.M.S.O., 1966, 24)

Renewed Attacks on the Cabinet Secretariat

The decision to route all League of Nations' paperwork through the Cabinet Secretariat rather than through the Foreign Office was one reason for the renewal of attacks upon the Cabinet Office (N.B. The terms 'Cabinet Office' and 'Cabinet Secretariat' are for most practical purposes interchangeable. Strictly the Cabinet Office comprises an Historical Section and, now, the Central Statistical Office, whose activities are described in Chapter IV, in addition to the Secretariat). Probably the root cause of most of the criticism was the refusal of some Conservatives to find anything good to say of any brain-child of Lloyd George. In fairness, however, there were two other factors disturbing even the unprejudiced onlooker.

First, few other than those at the heart of the Government machine knew precisely what the functions of the Secretariat were. One M.P. in a debate on the Cabinet Office (13 June 1922) remarked that it reminded him of the medical lecturer's words to his students: 'This is the spleen. We know nothing about the spleen. So much for the spleen.' Lord Gladstone, writing to *The Times* after the debate, challenged anyone to give from the speeches

of Mr Chamberlain and Mr Lloyd George a clear, connected account of what the Secretariat was or did. A
second reason for genuine concern was the growing cost
of the Secretariat services, as shown in the annual Votes.
Here are some relevant figures: 1917—£3,875; 1919—
£10,000; 1921—£35,000 (including a 50% salary increase
for Hankey from £2,000 to £3,000); 1922—£41,000 (including the cost of the Committee of Imperial Defence).
The debate just referred to did in fact occur during a
Supply debate on a motion to reduce by £100 the sum
allocated to the Cabinet Secretariat. Although speakers
in support of the motion included Isaac Foot and ex-
Premier Asquith amongst others, it was defeated by 205
votes to 113. The Government's case was strengthened by
the Geddes Report on National Expenditure that had just
appeared, which expressed the opinion that 'The amount
of work devolving upon this office [The Cabinet Secretariat]
is still very heavy and the Treasury, who have carefully
reviewed the whole staff from time to time are satisfied
that it is not in excess of what is required. In these circumstances we make no recommendations.' (Incidentally,
this Report gave the establishment of the Office as then
being—Administrative 11, Clerical 47, Typing 22, Messen-
gers 20, Cleaners 14—Total 114.)

The 1922 Election Campaign

Despite the vote of confidence mentioned above, the
Government did not receive a good press concerning its
defence of the Secretariat. *The Manchester Guardian*, *The
Times* and periodicals such as the *Spectator* and the *Nation*
were among those journals expressing their discontent. It
was therefore not surprising that when a few months later
the Conservatives suddenly broke from the Coalition
Government and thereby forced a general election they

should attack the Cabinet Office as part of their election campaign strategy.

Bonar Law, the new Prime Minister, made the opening speech of the campaign at St Andrews Hall, Glasgow. In his speech he said, 'We have decided to bring the Cabinet Secretariat system to an end'. ('Cheers!'). Elaborating his proposals he went on to say, 'I am convinced that the work can be done quite efficiently and far more economically by having the Cabinet Secretary and whatever help he needs, treated as part of the Treasury, which is the central department of Government. The work of the League of Nations which has hitherto been done by the Cabinet Secretariat shall be transferred to its proper place, the Foreign Office.' *The Times*, now under the control of Astor, not Northcliffe, commented on these remarks next day, 'The new Prime Minister could not have begun his election address more satisfactorily than by announcing his determination to put an end to the Cabinet Secretariat in its present form.

'Among the innovations of the Coalition Government none was less justified than the development of the so-called Cabinet Secretariat, which, in practice, became a Prime Ministerial department for the conduct of important national affairs apart from, or even in subversion of, well-tried constitutional practices and safeguards.' (*The Times*, 27 October 1922)

Careful reading of the above quotations will show that neither Law nor *The Times* explicitly advocated the complete abolition of the Secretariat, but only its curtailment. And this was just what was done by the Conservative Prime Ministers (Law and then Baldwin, after the former's resignation in May 1923 owing to cancer). They ended Lloyd George's 'Garden Suburb', transferred all League of Nations' secretarial work to the Foreign Office and reduced the Cabinet Office staff from 114 in 1922 to 38 in 1923. Certainly a drastic curtailment, although explained

29

in part by transfers to the Foreign Office of the relevant staff. What was more significant than the axing itself however was the implication that a Cabinet Office of sorts was not to be regarded as a war-time make-shift measure but as an integral permanent feature of the British Constitution. Cabinet Office personnel were placed under the Treasury as regards presentation of Estimates for Parliamentary approval, but in scarcely any other way could it be claimed that in practice they were subordinate to the Treasury, despite the efforts of Warren Fisher, Permanent Secretary to the Treasury, to bring this about. Hankey's independent authority was further emphasized by his additional appointment in 1923 as Secretary to the Privy Council. Top civil servant in the Cabinet Office, the Committee of Imperial Defence and in the Privy Council, he was well placed to defend his bailiwicks from any encroachments by the Treasury mandarins. Indeed, he held all three posts until his resignation in July 1938. Yet throughout his thirty years of public service this remarkable man continued to regard himself as an officer of the Royal Marines seconded for duty, rather than as a civil servant chary of Treasury autocracy.

3

Between the wars

The purpose of this chapter is to refer to certain well-known events in British politics from 1923 to 1938, and see how such matters were dealt with by the Cabinet Secretariat. One cannot go beyond 1938 since at the time of writing, Cabinet records after that year were not available to the general public. The events selected from this period are: the Campbell incident in 1924 which led to the precipitate downfall of the first Labour Government; the General Strike of 1926; and the economic crisis of 1931 which resulted in the formation of the National Government, Britain's only peace-time Coalition Government of this century. Finally there is a small section illustrating the large number of Cabinet Papers circulated by the Secretariat and the range of issues they cover.

1924: The Campbell Incident

Rather to the surprise of its leaders, the first-ever Labour Government came into office in January 1924, although Labour had not won the general election held in December 1923. The distribution of seats in Parliament resulting from that election was: Conservative 259, Labour 191, Liberal 159, others 6. The main issue of the election campaign had concerned imports and the rival merits of a policy of Protection or Free Trade. As both Labour and Liberal parties were united in supporting free trade, the Conservative Prime Minister, Baldwin, decided after certain hesitation that it would be pointless to stay in office and so resigned. King George V then invited Ramsay MacDonald, the Leader of the Labour Party, to become Prime Minister, which offer MacDonald accepted. In such a tenuous situation it was not surprising that this Labour Government held office for only a few months, but the occasion which led to its downfall still astonishes, forty-five years later. The main circumstances are given below:

On 25 July 1924, in a period of industrial unrest, an article appeared in the *Workers' Weekly* urging British soldiers 'neither in the class war nor the military war' to turn their guns on their fellow workers. On 6 August the Attorney-General, Sir Patrick Hastings, said in answer to questions in Parliament that the Government was intending to prosecute under the 1795 Incitement to Mutiny Act, John Campbell, the acting editor of the *Workers' Weekly* and, as such, the man responsible for the article.

This announcement brought consternation to Labour back-benchers and apparently to the Prime Minister himself. A Cabinet meeting was hurriedly called for that same evening, attended also by Hastings who, next morning, told the Director of Public Prosecutions that the charge against Campbell would be dropped. This decision to abandon the case led in turn to questions by Conservatives and Liberals as to why the Government had changed its mind, the inference being that it had allowed political considerations to nullify the normal process of law. The Liberals and the Conservatives tabled a motion that a Select Committee be appointed to enquire into the whole business but MacDonald would not agree to this proposal and a debate followed in which the Labour Government was defeated by 364 votes to 198. MacDonald immediately asked King George V to dissolve Parliament and in the ensuing election Labour was defeated and the Conservatives returned to office. The election was also a disaster, maybe a permanent one, for the Liberal Party which lost 118 seats, and up to 1969, at least, has never recovered the ground.

Clearly the decision to withdraw Campbell's prosecution taken at the Cabinet meeting on 6 August was a significant one affecting the political future of both the Labour and Liberal parties and it is interesting to see exactly what records of so historic a meeting were kept by the Secretariat. In the event, these records seem both fascinating and bewildering. Fascinating because they include first, a rarity amongst public Cabinet records, viz: a transcription of exchanges taken down there and then by Tom Jones, and second, a subsequent assertion by the Prime Minister of inaccuracy in the minutes; bewildering because as I read the records, the final decisions were not crystal clear. The reader may judge for himself. Here is the transcript made by Tom Jones (only the names of the offices held by the various speakers have been added).

Telegram from *Workers' Weekly* demanding resignation of Henderson.

Webb (President of Board of Trade). Director of Public Prosecution had applied to Hastings.

Prime Minister. First I heard in House of Commons Ammon said he's had a Minute from Admiralty. War Office agreed. Air agreed and Admiralty asked for views. He minuted against it. But I said 'It will not be begun until I know'. You add 'P.M. must be informed before action taken.' In papers I read it—done.

Snowdon (Chancellor of the Exchequer). Had been done then.

P.M. I sent for Assistant Director Public Prosecution. I asked him to take files on which he acted. Hastings said he did not authorize action. He was asked and said article criminal. Gave legal view. Assistant

Director saw me—he produced Minute. S. of S. agrees to go on with prosecution.

Henderson (Home Secretary). No. We agreed to transfer letters we'd received to the Director of Public Prosecution—two documents—printer and one from Creedy. Nothing about prosecution. I saw A. G. if he'd authorized proceedings. He agreed with you. He is under A. G. not under me.

P.M. I misread Minute also.

Henderson. My Secretary has known for a week that I was opposed to prosecution.

P.M. No-one agreed?

Henderson. I said it was criminal. I said got letter apology from printer who are cancelling . . . Hastings said I'll write telling Director not to proceed against printer.

Chelmsford (First Lord of the Admiralty). I had papers this a.m. with Ammon's note. I noted : I think we may agree with two Secretaries because Home Office will watch matter.

Walsh (War Minister). Papers brought to me by Adjutant-General and Creedy a few days ago. I went over Articles. Certain words were calculated to sow sedition. I minuted in my opinion a prosecution ought to lie. We've no power to prosecute.

Parmoor (Lord President). Entire responsibility with Attorney-General.

P.M. In case political should come to me.

(*Haldane* Royal Commission to give assent to Bill at 11.30. Exit Haldane)

J. H. Thomas (Colonial Secretary). Nothing of this sort should happen without P.M. and Cabinet knowing of it.

Parmoor. Attorney-General is responsible officer and ought not to act without consulting.

P.M. Not enough to give *legal* . . .

Wheatley. I think the Attorney-General feels he has more responsibility than legal.

J. H. T. The answer he gave in the House was . . .

Thomson (Air Minister). Yes.

P.M. Nothing except against Editor. He'll do nothing more.

(Enter Attorney-General)

Attorney-General (Hastings). Temporarily taken on post of Editor—someone on holiday—if desire not to press prosecution that might be opening for Prosecuting Counsel. It would drop then. I have informally had word with one concerned with Debate tonight. Make it difficult for criminal. So may get word debate won't go . . .

J. H. T. Create lively situation. Think they had got us on the run. Under whose authority . . .

Attorney-General. Gave an account of origin of case.

(Exit Henderson)

Bad criminal offence disclosed. Responsibility rests with me and I take it.

Parmoor. Ought you not to have consulted Prime Minister.

Attorney-General. Unfortunately there were two documents which rather looked as if there had been agreement. In case of great importance should go to Prime Minister.

Wedgwood (Duchy of Lancaster). Like Crowsley case— railway fireman. Used 1797 incitement to mutiny. He got two years.

Attorney-General. Exceptionally bad article.

Walsh. Communication I signed did not direct prosecution. Rested with others.

Attorney-General. I should again advise prosecution, but there is a possible way out if you desire it as against this man.

Thomson. I don't remember the case at all.

Prime Minister. Settled that no-one else will be arrested —I'd rather go through once started than show white feather. If you stop prosecution you will be asked all round what going to do. Editor is known—why not arrest him.

Walsh. Worst article I've ever read. One paragraph atrocious. I thought it would come before Cabinet. It would be peculiarly weak action if we abandoned prosecution having regard to all the circumstances.

J. H. Thomas. I move that it be an instruction that no prosecution of a political character take place without prior sanction of Cabinet.

(All agreed)

Prime Minister. If put to me I should not have sanctioned it. I know the men and the game. Now in press and House of Commons. Answer given.

J. H. Thomas. Don't withdraw now in view of House of Commons.

Wedgwood. Can you shift Public Prosecutor.

Snowdon. Both hands up for that.

Prime Minister. I'd like to see that Minute again. Initial Secretary P.S.

Henderson. My initials not on. When my Secretary sent letter over proceedings were taken.

Attorney-General. Director Public Prosecution got documents signed by Army Council to Home Office and back.

Wedgwood. Who started it?

Prime Minister reads paragraph 'Flesh of our Flesh' etc., from *Workers' Weekly*.

J. H. Thomas. Tripe.

Attorney-General. No debate tonight or tomorrow. Man arrested prepared to write letter to say he was only few days.

J. H. Thomas. Real fight will start two months hence.

Attorney-General. I'll accept his letter—reply being we had to take cognisance reluctantly.

Henderson. More questions tomorrow.

Attorney-General. Steps have been taken. Nothing to add. (Cab. 23-48, 453-457)

This remarkable dialogue was 'noted' by the acting Secretary in the following words:

The attention of the Cabinet was called to a prosecution which had been instituted against John Ross Campbell, Editor of the *Workers' Weekly*, the official organ of the Communist Party of Great Britain, under the Incitement to Mutiny Act, for attempting to seduce from loyalty to the King members of the Navy, Army and Air Force who might read the articles in the *Workers' Weekly* entitled 'The Army and Industrial Disputes'.

The Home Secretary stated that a letter of apology had been received from the printers, who are giving notice to terminate their printing contract, and he understood the

Attorney-General had given instructions that the printers should not be proceeded against.

The Attorney-General said he took full responsibility for proceeding with the case, which disclosed a bad criminal offence, but inasmuch as it transpired that the person charged was only acting temporarily as Editor and was prepared to write a letter to that effect, steps could be taken not to press the prosecution in the circumstances against this particular offender, if the Cabinet so desired.

After considerable discussion of the procedure which had led to action being taken in the Courts without the knowledge of the Cabinet or the Prime Minister the Cabinet agreed :

(a) that no public prosecution of a political character should be undertaken without the prior sanction of the Cabinet being obtained :

(b) That in the particular case under review the course indicated by the Attorney-General should be adopted. (Cab. 23-48, 467)

To me the crucial sentence is Hastings' reported statement that 'steps could be taken not to press the prosecution . . . if the Cabinet so desired.' Note the word is 'could' not 'would'. Then consider the wording of conclusion (b) . . . 'the course indicated by the Attorney-General should be adopted.' But which course is 'indicated'? The meaning, I suggest, is not clear. And my puzzlement increased when I discovered the two following notes in the records, each written in Hankey's own hand :

(i) On 22 September 1924, the Prime Minister, in the presence of a number of his Cabinet colleagues, asked me to show him the Cabinet conclusion in regard to the Prosecution of the Editor of the *Workers' Weekly* (Cabinet 48(24) conclusion 5 of August 6, 1924, 6 p.m.) On reading the Minute the Prime Minister at once challenged its accuracy, more particularly in regard to conclusion (b).

I made no record of this at the time, nor of the reasons given by the Prime Minister for this challenge, but, on returning to my office I mentioned to my private Secretary, Captain Burgis, that the Prime Minister had questioned the accuracy of the Minute, and I am asking Captain Burgis to initial this to bear out my statement.

> (signed) M. P. A. Hankey (Cab. 23-48, 451)

2 October 1924

(ii) The Prime Minister (Mr Ramsay MacDonald) asked me today to be sure that, if ever the Cabinet Minute 48(24) of 6 August 1924, 6 p.m., should be called for, I should also bring to notice the attached transcript of the notes made at the meeting by Mr T. Jones.
Replied that I would file a copy of the notes with the standard copy of the Cabinet conclusions.

> (Signed) M. P. A. Hankey (Cab. 23-48, 452)

3 November 1924

The statement that the Prime Minister challenged the accuracy of conclusion (b) implies that to him at least its meaning was plain even if incorrect. To me the words convey an aura of ambiguity which seems so contrary to the normal pattern of Cabinet conclusions.

Finally, what is one to make of MacDonald's categorical statement in the House of Commons on 30 September: 'I was not consulted regarding either the institution or the subsequent withdrawal of these proceedings. I never advised its withdrawal but left the whole matter to the discretion of the Law Officers, where that discretion properly rests'? Or of the Attorney-General's remarks also in the House, 'All I can say is that I left the Cabinet meeting [on 6 August] with a decision at which I had arrived interfered with by nobody'?

One thing which is factually certain is that the new Conservative Government which succeeded MacDonald's, made no attempt to pursue the Campbell case any further. The Cabinet Minute recording this is rather neatly worded:

As the late Prime Minister rather than submit to an inquiry had deliberately appealed to the verdict of the
country which had been given at the recent General Election, the circumstances in which the last Parliament had
voted for an Inquiry were changed and an Inquiry by
Select Committee or otherwise was not now desirable or in
the public interest.

Such is the logic of political leadership.

The General Strike 1926

Many books have been written about the ten days in May
1926, when nearly all the trade unions were on strike in
support of the miners, who were threatened with a wage
reduction. This is not the place to recapitulate, however
sketchily, the main events in that industrial dispute. What
I have done is to select one or two relevant extracts from
Cabinet minutes of the meetings on the eventful Sunday,
2 May 1926, when last minute efforts were being made to
avert the strike. Inevitably when crises occur calling for
speedy Cabinet action, the strain on the Secretariat becomes intense. On this Sunday, there were three separate
Cabinet meetings held and altogether it required eleven
type-written foolscap sheets to record the day's proceedings. Anyone who has had to summarize, within a few
hours, one important discussion with about twenty
participants will appreciate the skill displayed by Hankey
and his men on this occasion.

First, a minute indicating the thoroughness with which
the Baldwin Government was preparing for any even-
tuality: 'The Cabinet agreed that the Postmaster General
should communicate to the Prime Minister copies of telegrams which had been sent by Trade Unions in connexion
with the order for a general strike'! (Cab. 23-52)

Next, an extract which, most unusually, was omitted
from the copies circulated to ministers but included in

the one copy sent to the King:

The general view of the Cabinet was that the above formula was too vague and indefinite, and gave no assurance that the proposed negotiations were likely to lead to a successful issue; and that taken in conjunction with the menace of a general strike, it would be regarded by public opinion as a yielding by the Government to threats. It was felt that negotiations involving the payment of a subsidy ought not to be resumed without a definite answer from the Miners in regard to their acceptance of the Report of the Royal Commission, which, of course, would commit the Miners to make some sacrifice as indicated in that Report.

It was assumed that in any event the complete withdrawal of the threat of a general strike was *sine qua non* to any resumption of negotiations involving a subsidy.

As regards the letter in Appendix II, the general opinion of the Cabinet was that it should either not be answered at all, or else a very stiff reply should be sent. Suggestions were made that in the event of a sympathetic general strike, as now contemplated, legislation should be introduced to remove the immunity of strike funds in such cases, and to make picketing illegal. (Cab. 23-52, 315-316)

The formula mentioned early on in this extract referred to a settlement of the coal dispute on the basis of the Report of the Royal Commission chaired by Sir Herbert Samuel. The letter in Appendix II mentioned in the minute was one by Citrine, Acting Secretary to the T.U.C. informing the government that, 'in the event of the strike . . . the General Council is prepared to enter into arrangements for the distribution of essential foodstuffs'. It is difficult to understand why the above quoted extract from Cabinet minutes was excluded from the copies sent to Cabinet members. The conclusions appear to be no more 'dangerous' than many others circulated to these secrecy-pledged Privy Councillors.

The final break-down of negotiations occurred late on

the Sunday night, when members of the National Association of Operative Printers and Assistants of the Daily Mail staff had refused to print an editorial concerning the strike. This was recorded by the Cabinet Secretary as follows:

A discussion by the Cabinet followed . . . Shortly after authentic information was received to the effect that certain employees in the office of the Daily Mail had declined to print a leading article and that the Daily Mail would not be published tomorrow.

This evidence, coupled with the evidence of specific instructions directing members of certain Trade Unions in several of the most vital services and industries of the country to carry out a General Strike on Tuesday next, was felt to introduce a new factor in the situation and it was agreed that negotiations could not be continued without a repudiation by the T.U.C. Committee of the actions referred to and an immediate and unconditional withdrawal of the instructions for a general strike. (Cab. 23-52)

The noncommittal phrase 'authentic information was received' refers, according to the historian A. J. P. Taylor, to news of the incident being telephoned to the Cabinet by the editor of the *Daily Mail*. Taylor goes on to suggest that the editor may have 'aimed deliberately at provocation, perhaps even with encouragement from inside the Cabinet'. (Taylor, 1965, 244)

During the course of the Strike attempts were made by Herbert Samuel to bring the two sides—miners and mine-owners—together. The Cabinet was determined to make it plain that any such overtures were entirely unofficial; exactly how determined the following extracts show. First, from a Cabinet Conclusion dated 8 May:

The Cabinet approved the terms of a confidential letter to be sent by the Minister of Labour to Sir H. Samuel, the Chairman of the Royal Commission into the Coal Industry 1925, who had returned from Italy and, on his own initiative and without any vestige of authority, had held some conversations with miners and mine-owners. (Cab. 23-52)

Next, here is the letter sent to Samuel in accordance with these instructions. It is worth quoting in full, if only to do justice to its polished phraseology.

8th May, 1926.

My dear Samuel,

It has occurred to me since our conversation this afternoon that in dealing with a matter so delicate it would be better to place upon record in writing the attitude of the government as I understand it.

We have repeatedly stated that we cannot negotiate until the General Strike has been withdrawn.

This statement has a very particular meaning. It means that until the necessary orders have been given to withdraw the Strike or unless the Strike has come to an end we cannot as a condition or inducement take part in negotiations in relation to the mining issue. For if we did so, there would and could be no *unconditional* withdrawal of the Strike notices. On the contrary, the true situation sincerely faced would be that we had procured the end of the General Strike by a process of bargaining. The consent to do this would in fact fatally disable the Government for a task which, as trustees of the community, they conceive themselves bound to undertake. Their position is plain. They hold that the General Strike is unconstitutional and illegal. They are bound to take steps to make its repetition impossible. It is therefore plain that they cannot enter upon any negotiations unless the strike is so unreservedly concluded that there is not even an implication of such a bargain upon their side as would embarrass them in any legislation which they may conceive to be proper in the light of recent events.

In these circumstances, I am sure that the Government will take the view that while they are bound most carefully and most sympathetically to consider the terms of any arrangement which a public man of your responsibility and experience may propose, it is imperative to make it plain that any discussion which you think proper to initiate is not clothed in even a vestige of official character.

Yours sincerely,
(Sgd) Arthur Steel Maitland
(Min. of Labour)

(Cab. 23-52, 361-362)

That last sentence is a gem. There can be no case here of honest doubt about the Cabinet's precise position.

Finally, a totally unimportant example of the Secretariat's deadpan style in recording top-level decisions: 'The Home Secretary should warn the Minister of Transport of the risk of sabotage by electrical workers, e.g. by dropping a spanner in some delicate part of machinery.' (Cab. 23-52)

The 1931 Political Crisis

Probably more has been written about this event, which resulted in the replacement of a Labour Government by a 'National' Government, than about any other issue of twentieth-century British peace-time politics. Much of the writing by Jennings, Samuel, and others, is contradictory, as is shown in R. Bassett's excellent account, *Nineteen Thirty One*. The crucial Cabinet meetings leading to the resignation of Ramsay MacDonald's Labour Government are recorded in a manner which conveys none of the atmosphere with which those meetings must have been charged. For instance, one would never infer from reading the minutes alone that when the Prime Minister read out to his colleagues the telegram in which the New York bankers declared their terms for a loan, it seemed to those outside that 'pandemonium had broken loose' within the Cabinet room. (Nicholson, 1952, 463)

Cabinet meetings were held every day from 19 to 24

August (two meetings on Saturday, 22 August) and the heavy strain on the Secretariat's reporting section can easily be imagined. This sentence of 150 words can be forgiven, one feels, since after all the meaning is clear:

After reminding the Cabinet that the Chancellor of the Exchequer and himself had seen the representatives of the Bank of England on the previous afternoon, and had ascertained from them that after getting in touch with Mr. Harrison they would communicate with him again, the Prime Minister informed the Cabinet that he had received at 10.0 p.m. on the previous evening a telephone message from Sir E. Harvey, to the effect that Mr. Harrison had expressed his own personal opinion that, if a further £20 millions gross was added to the list of economies, made up as to £12¼ millions by a 10 per cent reduction in Unemployment Insurance benefit and as to £7¾ millions in other ways, the proposals as a whole would be satisfactory from the point of view of the proposed loan, but that he must first confer with the financial interests responsible for raising the money in New York. (Cab. 23-67, 356)

The vital meeting was on Sunday evening, 23 August, begun at 7.00 p.m. and adjourned at 7.45 p.m., to await a message from America as to whether a loan might be obtainable and if so on what terms. It is said that during this adjournment which lasted for about an hour and a quarter with the ministers pacing the garden of No. 10 in the summer evening, Henderson did what he could do to dissuade his colleagues from accepting any terms which would result in a cut in unemployment relief payments. (Nicholson, 1952, 462) When the meeting was continued at 9.10 p.m., and the terms put before the Cabinet, a vote was taken with nine of the twenty members opposing acceptance of the loan. This may well be fact but, of course, none of it was recorded by the Cabinet Secretary. The minutes summarize the Premier's arguments for accepting the American loan and then continue:

In conclusion, the Prime Minister said that it must be admitted that the proposals as a whole, represented the negation of everything that the Labour Party stood for, and yet he was absolutely satisfied that it was necessary in the national interests, to implement them if the country was to be secured. He then pointed out that, if on this question there were any important resignations, the Government as a whole must resign.

Each member of the Cabinet then expressed his views on the question of the inclusion, or otherwise, in the proposals, of the 10 per cent reduction in Unemployment Insurance benefit. In the course of these expressions of view, indications were given that, while a majority of the Cabinet favoured the inclusion in the economy proposals of the 10 per cent reduction in unemployment insurance benefit, the adoption of this as part and parcel of the scheme would involve the resignation of certain Ministers from the Government.

In these circumstances the Prime Minister informed the Cabinet that he proposed to acquaint His Majesty at once with the situation which had arisen, and to advise him to hold a conference with Mr Baldwin, Sir H. Samuel and himself on the following morning. The Cabinet agreed to this proposal, and also authorized the Prime Minister to inform His Majesty that all Cabinet Ministers had placed their resignations in the Prime Minister's hands. The Prime Minister left the meeting of the Cabinet at 10.10 p.m.

The Prime Minister returned from Buckingham Palace at about 10.40 p.m. and stated to the Cabinet that he had informed His Majesty of the situation, namely that, while the Government had agreed that the Budget should be balanced, they had been unable to reach agreement on proposals to deal effectively with the existing financial emergency, and accordingly that it was impossible for them to continue in office as a united Cabinet. He had then advised His Majesty that he should accord an Audience to Mr Baldwin, Sir Herbert Samuel and himself on the following morning, and his Majesty had been pleased to fix 10 a.m. as the time for this Audience.

The Cabinet agreed:

(i) That no announcement should be issued to the Press;

(ii) That the Prime Minister should inform the Leaders of the Opposition Parties forthwith of the nature of the message which he had received from Mr Harrison;

(iii) To leave the question of the summoning of Parliament in the hands of the Prime Minister;

(iv) That a further meeting of the Cabinet should be held on Monday next, August 24th, 1931, at No. 10 Downing Street, at 12 noon, but that no formal notice of this meeting should be issued. (Cab. 23-67, 360-362)

Varying versions have been given and different interpretations made both of the audience next morning which King George V gave to the three party leaders, and of the Cabinet meeting immediately following that audience. Here is MacDonald's own account given to his Cabinet colleagues at the Cabinet meeting held on Monday, 24 August, as reported by the Cabinet Secretary:

The Prime Minister informed the Cabinet that, as a result of the failure to reach agreement on the previous day, the financial position had greatly deteriorated, and the situation was now one of the gravest possible character.

As had then been arranged, His Majesty had received Mr Baldwin, Sir Herbert Samuel and himself in audience that morning, and it was quite clear that no useful purpose would be served by consideration of any question other than that of saving the country from financial collapse. The proposal was that His Majesty would invite certain individuals, as individuals, to take upon their shoulders the burden of carrying on the Government, and Mr Baldwin and Sir Herbert Samuel had stated that they were prepared to act accordingly.

The Prime Minister then stated that he proposed to tender to His Majesty the resignation of the Government. He had not failed to present the case against his participation in the proposed Administration, but in view of the gravity of the situation he had felt that there was no other course open to him than to assist in the formation of a National Government on a comprehensive basis for

46

the purpose of meeting the present emergency.

The new Cabinet would be a very small one of about 12 Ministers, and the Administration would not exist for a period longer than was necessary to dispose of the emergency, and when that purpose was achieved the political parties would resume their respective positions. The Administration would not be a Coalition Government in the usual sense of the term but a Government of co-operation for this one purpose. (Cab. 23-67, 367-368)

Unfortunately the Cabinet minutes record the rest of this historic meeting only in bald factual terms referring to the proposed date of any forthcoming General Election; provision for the retention of Cabinet documents should any minister so wish; and the surrendering of seals of office. Rather surprisingly the third and last item of the meeting is minuted as follows: 'On the motion of the Lord Chancellor, the Cabinet placed on record their warm appreciation of the great kindness, consideration and courtesy invariably shown by the Prime Minister when presiding over their meetings and conducting the business of the Cabinet.' (Cab. 23-67, 371)

To the historian, as well as the journalist, facts are sacred. But facts in themselves may only provide half-truths as the Secretary's official account of this meeting shows. No hint is given of the tension in the atmosphere or the emotions engendered by the Premier's account of the events of that morning's rendezvous at Buckingham Palace. Morrison, the youngest member of the Cabinet, has told how he and his colleagues were 'shocked and nonplussed' by MacDonald's words. (Morrison, 1960, 126) After a pause and a low whistle of astonishment from Henderson, Morrison was the first to speak. 'Prime Minister,' he said, 'I think you are wrong,' to which MacDonald snapped 'You think I am wrong.' (Morrison, 1960, 127) Bassett observes that, 'In commentary after commentary it has been said that when MacDonald announced that a National Government was to be formed under his leadership, his Cabinet colleagues were stunned —rendered almost speechless with amazement.' (Bassett, 1958, 158) Henderson left the Cabinet Room almost 'too shattered to speak' according to another account. (Bassett, 1958, 158) Knowledge of these reactions is vital for a full awareness of the drama of the occasion. However, Cabinet Secretaries are recorders not dramatists. Their job is to provide an accurate account of decisions taken, and not to portray scenes of passions aroused. But it all reminds one of Pilate's question, 'What is truth?'

Immediately on taking office the new un-Keynesian National Government set about cutting down public expenditure with grim determination. Anyone associated with the field of public education will find something disturbingly familiar in their proposals to economize on teachers' salaries, which were in fact reduced by 10 per cent. The question arose as to how soon the cut could be imposed, assuming, that is, one had some regard for the sanctity of legal contracts. On this point the Cabinet discussion which follows is illuminating:

Arising out of a consideration of the proposed economies in expenditure on Education in England and Wales, the Cabinet discussed at some length the date at which the scheme of economies was to be brought into operation.

It was explained that, so far as the Board of Education was concerned, the question of the date was governed by the contracts of the teachers. These contracts, which were entered into, not by the State but by the Local Education Authorities (to whom the State pays a percentage grant), provided, in the event of a change in conditions, for notice which varied from one month to six. The Burnham Scale, on which the rates of pay were based, was a contractual obligation, enforceable in a Court of Law, which made it impossible to abrogate the rates summarily. An alteration in the conditions of contracts would require a good deal of negotiation. Such negotiations were far more likely to result in a durable settlement if they could be dealt with as a whole, that is to say, if the date of operation of the economies, so far as the teachers were concerned, could be postponed until April 1st.

The President of the Board of Education intimated that some small economies could be effected in the current financial year if the date of commencement was fixed at January 1st, 1932, but this would involve great administrative confusion, and he could not recommend it, particularly in view of the relatively small economies that could be realized in the present financial year. January 1st was the earliest date at which economies could begin to operate, and he emphasized that on a long view there were great advantages in commencing all the new contracts on the same date.

The postponement of the date for commencement of economies until January 1st, and still more until April 1st, in the case of the Board of Education, was found to present overwhelming objections from the point of view of the scheme of economies as a whole. From the political and psychological aspect the Cabinet felt strongly that in the present grave national emergency it was important to put the scheme into operation at the earliest date and, as far as possible, as a whole. The Fighting Services hoped to be able to begin their economies on pay, cost of living and pensions from October 1st, provided that the Cabinet took a decision without delay, but the Ministers concerned advised that the personnel affected could only be induced to accept the reductions involved if assured that it was essential to the salvation of the country *and provided that equal sacrifices were made by all branches of the public service.* This latter consideration applied equally to the police forces. The exemption of one branch of the public service was calculated greatly to increase the difficulty of securing acceptance in other branches. The Cabinet felt also that the moral right of the Fighting Services and the Police to regard their conditions of pay and pensions as a contract, even though it was not enforceable in a Court of Law, was not inferior to that of the teachers.

Various suggestions were made as to how the difficulties of the President of the Board of Education might be overcome. One such suggestion was to make the teachers' cuts in some way retrospective. Thus, as a condition of their new contracts, they might have to make up the balance next year, or they might be given the option, either of accepting voluntarily the reduction in their salaries at once, or of foregoing later on a corresponding amount. Political objections to this course were pointed out. Another suggestion was that all branches of the public service incurring cuts in salaries, wages or pay, including teachers, might be given a note stating the amount due to them on their present scale, together with the sum to be deducted owing to the present financial emergency. By this means the money would be obtained at once; there would be no question of a breach of contract; and time would be gained for negotiations for a more permanent settlement. This latter course, however, was found to be open to considerable objections. For example, it would greatly increase the difficulties of giving any degree of permanence to the reductions even in the case of classes of public servants who are notoriously over-paid, and would lead to demands for re-instatement of the original amount. The proposal was rejected.

The President of the Board of Education, while emphasizing the great difficulties involved in upsetting existing legislation and contracts without having time to conduct the necessary negotiations (in which connection he instanced the complication of the voluntary schools), undertook to do his best to meet the desire of the Cabinet that teachers' economies should be on the same basis as those affecting the Fighting Services and the Police (notwithstanding the difference in the contractual relation of teachers to the State), and should take effect as from October 1st. The Prime Minister said that the Cabinet fully appreciated the difficulties of the President of the Board of Education, and would do their best to assist him in carrying out their decision.

The Cabinet agreed:

That the date at which economies in salaries, pay

and pensions should begin to operate should be
October 1st, 1931. (Cab. 23-68, 23-26)

Cabinet Papers

Most issues requiring Cabinet decision are accompanied
by explanatory memoranda and an important part of
any Cabinet minister's routine is to ensure that he has
done his homework and comes to each Cabinet meeting
fully briefed on every agenda item. The circulation,
control and indexing of this paper-work is the job of the
Cabinet Office. This is easy to say, but to convey some
idea of the work involved, here is a list of topics covered
by separate Cabinet papers circulated during December
1937. (There is nothing special about this date—at the
time of writing it just happens to be the last month for
which records are available to the public. In the thirty
years since then, the output of paper-work has almost
certainly increased):

Policy in Palestine (three separate papers); an appreciation of the political situation in India; A.R.P. in Schools;
Amendments to the N.H. Insurance Act; regulation of
wages in the Transport of Goods by Roads; Hire Purchase
Bill; Comparison of the strength of Great Britain with
that of certain other Nations (sic) as at January 1938; the
situation in the Mediterranean and Middle East; relations
with the Irish Free State; withdrawal of British troops
from Shanghai; British News abroad (a review by Foreign
Secretary Eden); refugee problem in Spain; establishment
of a Civil Air Licensing Authority in U.K.; re-organization
of the Cotton Industry; Licensing of Advertisements Bill;
Prevention and Treatment of Blindness Bill; Pensions for
M.P.s; protection of Vital Services (a memorandum from
the Minister for Co-ordination of Defence); Divorce and
Nullity of Marriage Bill; share pushing; shipping—Com-
petition of Matson Line against British Lines; reform of

League of Nations; defence expenditure in future years; proposed appointment of Irish Free State Minister in Rome; State of Trade.

Small wonder that a period of service within the Cabinet Office is considered to be valuable training for any promising high-flyer in the Civil Service. It should certainly eliminate parochial partiality.

4

The war and post-war period

Unfortunately for the student of Whitehall politics, the proceedings of Cabinet and Cabinet committee meetings during and after the Second World War are not available to the general public, and so information has to be gleaned from other sources. But before we come to the war years there is one event which can and should be mentioned. This is the resignation of Hankey on his reaching the age of sixty in July 1938. He was succeeded by Sir Edward Bridges, son of a former Poet Laureate. Sir Robert Howorth, Deputy Secretary to the Cabinet, became in addition Secretary to the Privy Council.

World War II

A student can read up the many biographies written by leading statesmen and warriors of the period, including, of course, Churchill's own incomparable account of these years. Even so, he will not find many factual references to the work of members of the Cabinet Office. However, perhaps a short list of some war-time Cabinet changes will convey an idea of the work behind the scenes which at times must have strained the Secretariat mightily. These changes included:

1939   On the outbreak of war Chamberlain reduced the size of his Cabinet from 21 to 9 (including Hankey, granted a peerage, as Minister without Portfolio). The Committee of Imperial Defence and its Secretariat were absorbed into the Cabinet and its Secretariat, as in 1916.

1940   May. Churchill replaced Chamberlain as Prime Minister and formed a War Cabinet consisting of himself in the joint roles of Prime Minister and Minister of Defence; Chamberlain, his predecessor, as Lord President; Attlee and Greenwood, both Labour men, as Lord Privy Seal and Minister without Portfolio respectively and Halifax as Foreign Secretary.

1940   October. The War Cabinet was enlarged by the inclusion of the Minister of Aircraft Production, the Chancellor of the Exchequer and the Minister of Labour.

        December. Halifax was appointed Ambassador in the U.S.A. but remained in the Cabinet. The new Foreign Secretary, Eden, also joined the Cabinet.

1941   Beaverbrook became Minister of Supply and remained in the Cabinet, but not so his replacement as Minister of Aircraft Production.

        A new post of Minister of State for the Middle East was created and the holder, Lyttelton, became a member of the Cabinet.

1942   The Ministry of Production was created. The Chancellor of Exchequer left the Cabinet. Lyttelton became Minister of Aircraft Production and remained in the Cabinet. His successor as Minister in the Middle East, Casey, an Australian M.P., also became a Cabinet member.

        Cripps resigned as Lord Privy Seal but his replacement was not in the Cabinet. The Home Secretary joined the Cabinet.

1943   Minister   for   Reconstruction   (Lord   Woolton)
       became a Cabinet member.

A bare account such as this can give little indication of the work involved for the Secretariat. Some of the background to the bald statement 'Ministry of Production was created' may illustrate this point. In the first place, in 1940, Churchill wanted Beaverbrook to take over Supply and Aircraft Production but the latter's asthma prevented his accepting these dual responsibilities. However, the Prime Minister still insisted on taking responsibility for aircraft production away from the Air Ministry and created a new department for this purpose the following year.

Beaverbrook was switched from the Ministry of Aircraft Production to the Ministry of Supply but this arrangement did not work out too well for there was much friction between these two departments. So in February 1942, Beaverbrook was appointed Minister of Production to co-ordinate Supply and Aircraft Production but no separate Ministry was created. Before the month was out, however, Beaverbrook had resigned the office partly because of 'his own doubts about the functions and powers of the new Office'. (Chester, 1957, 234) (He had won control of War Transport from Leathers but failed to gain an inch of territory from Bevin, Ministry of Labour and National Service. There was strong ill-feeling between Beaverbrook and Bevin.) Beaverbrook was replaced by Lyttelton, who was determined to give his office 'greater substance and definition than it appeared to possess at the outset'. (Chester, 1957, 235)

Finally, after much dissension behind the scenes, a Ministry of Production was established in July 1942, which took over from the Ministry of Supply responsibilities in connection with raw materials and machine tools. One can only guess at the innumerable papers, committee meetings etc., caused by these administrative changes and efficiently served by members of the ubiquitous Cabinet Secretariat. Certainly it was Bridges in person who delivered to Beaverbrook Churchill's ultimatum of 10 February 1942, offering him for the last time the post of Minister of Production, which offer Beaverbrook accepted, though with many misgivings. It is hard to believe that the Secretary of the Cabinet was here being personally used in the capacity of post boy and nothing else.

As in the First World War, numerous Cabinet and ministerial committees were formed to help reduce the load on the War Cabinet and enable it principally to concentrate on the prosecution of the war. During the 1920s and 1930s the only standing Cabinet Committee had been the Home Affairs Committee which, despite its impressive title was concerned with little else than the vetting of bills about to be presented to Parliament. But Churchill soon altered the scene. Concerning military matters there were the Defence Committee (Operations) and the Defence Committee (Supply), as well as Chiefs of Staff Committee and regular meetings of the Vice-Chiefs of Staff. (The Chiefs of Staff Committee alone averaged over 400 meetings each year.) (Taylor, 1965, 482) As for civilian affairs, there was the important Lord President's Committee which, under Sir John Anderson's chairmanship, became extremely influential, co-ordinating committees on Economic Policy, Civil Defence, Food Production etc. All these committees were serviced by members of the Cabinet Secretariat.

A rich source of snippets which indicate in some detail the range of the Cabinet Secretariat's wartime activities, both civil and military, is the memoirs of Churchill, especially as these often convey so well the flavour of the man. The directives which came Bridges' way (known colloquially as prayers, so often did they begin 'Pray let me have your views. . . .' or 'Pray explain . . .' etc.) covered an incredible diversity of topics as the following selection illustrates: control of timber supplies, safety of secret documents, vulnerability of Whitehall to air attack, centralizing of Government statistics, exchange of prisoners of war, the political situation in India, the organization of Scientific Research, the ringing of church bells, the case for 'Basic English', housing in the post-war transitional period, cottages for agricultural labourers, etc. One communication to the Cabinet Office, supporting the retention of some fighter aircraft by the R.A.F. rather than allowing them to be transferred to the Fleet Air Arm, included this warning observation from Churchill, himself an ex-First Lord of the Admiralty, 'The Admiralty always want not only to win the game but to go to bed with the ace'. (Churchill, 1951, 788) One or two examples of minutes from the Prime Minister to the Cabinet Secretary are worth quoting in full:

19 July 1940
Let it be very clearly understood that all directions emanating from me are made in writing, and that I do not accept any responsibility for matters relating to national defence on which I am alleged to have given decisions unless they are recorded in writing. (Churchill, 1949, 17)

11 July 1941
Take the Hansards of the two days' production debate and have all the passages which effect particular departments extracted and sent to the departments concerned with a request for their answers by July 19th.

Also pick out any passages which affect the central direction of the war and let me have them.

It seems to me there were a lot of very good points made. (Churchill, 1950, 716)

27 February 1942
The Cabinet arrangements for next week should be as follows:
1 Monday, 5.30 p.m. at No. 10. General Parade with the Constant Attenders, the Chiefs of Staff, and the Dominions and India representatives. Business: the

general war situation, without reference to special secret matters such as forthcoming operations; and any other appropriate topics.

2 Tuesday, 6 p.m. at No. 10. Pacific Council.

3 Wednesday, 12 noon at House of Commons. War Cabinet only, with yourself. We summon anyone we need for particular pages.

4 Thursday, 12 noon, at House of Commons. War Cabinet. (On both Wednesday and Thursday if the business requires it, another meeting will be held at 6 p.m.)

5 Friday, 10 p.m. Defence Committee. This will consist of the Chiefs of Staff, Service Ministers, India and Dominions, if and as required, myself, the Deputy Prime Minister and the Foreign Secretary and probably Mr Oliver Lyttelton.

Let us see how this works. (Churchill, 1951, 78)

14 July 1943
The Public Relations Officers are becoming a scandal and the whole system requires searching, pointing and drastic pruning. Pray advise me how to proceed. A small Cabinet committee with a suitable reference would seem to be indicated. (Churchill, 1952, 573)

These examples refer to matters concerning the Home Front. But the Secretariat was also much involved with the prosecution of the war itself since, as has been said, the Committee of Imperial Defence Secretariat was merged with the Cabinet Secretariat on the outbreak of war in 1939. Furthermore, Churchill, on becoming Prime Minister, also appointed himself Minister for Defence but did not create a Defence Ministry. Instead, for most practical purposes he used the services of the former Committee of Imperial Defence personnel. Head of these was General Ismay, who acted in a kind of dual capacity as Military Secretary to the Cabinet and Chief Staff Officer to Mr Churchill. To quote Ismay's own words; 'It is not easy to define my precise position in relation to my chief. His own description of me as "the head of his handling machine" seems pretty near the mark, but I prefer the term "Agent". Anyhow, that is how I interpreted the part.' (Ismay, 1960, 168) The consequence was that the military staff of the Secretariat were probably even more subject to Churchillian pressures than were their civilian counterparts. There was, for example, this minute of 2 August 1940, to General Ismay, headed ominously 'Action this day':

1 Next week one of my principal tasks must be going through this scheme of the Air Ministry for increasing the pilots and for the training of pilots. Lord Beaverbrook should be asked for his views beforehand.
2 Let me have a report on the plans for lectures on tactical subjects for the troops in the autumn.
3 What has been done about the collection of scrap of all kinds? Let me have a short report on one page covering the progress made this year.
4 When at the Admiralty I took a special interest in the work of the Salvage Department and held a meeting there four months ago. A naval officer, Captain Dewar, was then in charge. Let me have a report on what has happened to salvage since that day.
5 I am also expecting this week to reach settlement about the functions of the A.R.P. and Police in the case of invasion. The Lord Privy Seal was dealing with this in the first instance. At the same time we must consider allowing transfers from the A.R.P. to the Home Guard and their being made available for fighting purposes. To what extent has the payment of A.R.P. personnel been discontinued or restricted? It ought to be continually restricted.
6 Let me have a report on the progress and future construction of tank divisions . . . Let me know also what are the latest ideas for the structure and organization of an armoured division. This should be prepared on one sheet of paper, showing all the principal elements and accessories.

Later that day, as if to ensure that there were no idle

hands round the Secretariat building, another missile came down from Olympus: 'It is very important to get on with the uniforms for the Home Guard. Let me have forecast of deliveries.' (Churchill, 1949, 575)

One feels that neither of the famous Churchillian injunctions—'Clarity and cogency can be reconciled with a greater brevity', nor 'It is slothful not to compress your thoughts'—would be necessary in Secretariat circles. In point of fact, Ismay's technique when ordered to compress a complex issue to 'one sheet of paper' was to present the fullest summary possible in that space and then attach the detailed information on which such summary was based in the form of appendices, A, B, C, etc. Churchill seemed to have no objection to this method, even when once Ismay reached Appendix T having spent two foolscap pages on one item alone. (Ismay, 1960, 169)

Ismay also travelled extensively either with or at the bidding of the Prime Minister. In 1941, he went with Lord Beaverbrook to Moscow. In early 1943 he was in Churchill's party at the 'Unconditional Surrender' conference in Casablanca. A report sent from there by Churchill to the War Cabinet and 'drawn up under my direction by General Ismay' on 20 January included the following:

We propose to draw up a statement of the work of the conference for communication to the Press at the proper time. I should be glad to know what the War Cabinet would think of our including in this statement a declaration of the firm intention of the United States and the British Empire to continue the war relentlessly until we have brought about the 'unconditional surrender' of Germany and Japan. The omission of Italy would be to encourage a break up there. (Churchill, 1951, 613)

That same day in London the Secretariat was able to arrange for this matter to be discussed at the afternoon Cabinet meeting and the next day the following reply was sent:

The Cabinet were unanimously of opinion that balance of advantage lay against excluding Italy, because of misgivings which would inevitably be caused in Turkey, in the Balkans and elsewhere. Nor are we convinced that effect on Italians would be good. Knowledge of all rough stuff coming to them is surely more likely to have the desired effect on Italian morale. (Churchill, 1951, 614)

On 24 January, at a Press Conference in Casablanca, President Roosevelt announced the Allies intention to force 'unconditional surrender' on all their enemies. It is surprising, given the existence of these two clearly written documents, to find Bevin, who was a War Cabinet member at that time, saying some years later in the House of Commons that the War Cabinet had never been consulted about 'the unconditional surrender' phrase. (H.C. Debates, 21 July 1949) Such a slip of memory, though undoubtedly made in good faith, is one more salutary reminder of how important it is to have an efficient Secretariat, not least in order to get the record straight.

Later in 1943 Ismay went to assist his masters at conferences in Quebec, Teheran, and Moscow. He was present at Yalta in 1944 (as also was Bridges) and Potsdam in 1945. Of course in all these visits he was acting more in his military capacity as member of the Chiefs of Staff Committee than as a Cabinet Secretary. Foreign Minister Eden amongst others has paid tribute to his military knowledge, how, for instance, Ismay was able to stand up to Marshall Voroshilov and other Russian military leaders, arguing point for point on factors such as supplies, transportation, strategy etc., when the Russians were opposing our insistence that a Second Front in Europe would have to be delayed until 1944.

It is doubtful if many people knew on V.E. Day, or know now how important a role was played by the Cabinet Secretariat members, military and civil, during the war years. To toast them in Churchillian style, as 'the architects of victory' might be an exaggeration but those at the centre appreciated their worth. It was a nice thought of King George VI's that he, Bridges and Ismay ought to be photographed together as the only three who had kept their jobs throughout the war. (Ismay, 1960, 396)

Post-War Changes

Very little information is available to the general public about the activities of the Cabinet Secretariat during the last two decades. In consequence, the student can only speculate on how much the resources of the Cabinet Office must have been strained by such events as the nationalization policies of the 1945/50 Labour Government or the 1956 Suez crisis, etc.

Two changes in personnel at the top level should be recorded. In 1945, Bridges was appointed Permanent Secretary to the Treasury, an appointment which carried with it also the status and responsibility of Head of the Home Civil Service. He agreed, however, to continue serving as Cabinet Secretary, but to relieve him of some of this extra burden, Norman Brook (later Lord Normanbrook) was appointed as an extra Secretary to the Cabinet. Brook had a deservedly high reputation in Whitehall circles, not least owing to his work as Secretary to Anderson's wartime Lord President's Committee, already mentioned. He had also been Deputy Secretary at the Cabinet Secretariat for a year before being chosen by Lord Woolton as Permanent Secretary to his new Ministry of Reconstruction in 1943. The volume of work however was still too heavy for Bridges. Consequently in 1947 he relinquished his official connection with the Secretariat and Brook became full Secretary to Cabinet. In 1956 Bridges retired, to be replaced by two Joint Permanent Secretaries to the Treasury, one in charge of finance and economic affairs, the other to be Head of the Civil Service and concerned with establishment matters within the Service. This latter post went to Brook who also continued, however, as Cabinet Secretary. In his own way, Brook was as remarkable and as talented a public servant as either of his predecessors, serving loyally and well four Prime Ministers— Attlee, Churchill, Eden and Macmillan—and acting as Secretary to nearly a dozen Commonwealth Prime Ministers' Meetings during his term of office.

When Brook retired in 1962, Premier Macmillan announced a further reorganization of these top level responsibilities, making a clear tripartite division of duties between (a) Joint Permanent Secretary of the Treasury concerned with the financial and economic work of that department; (b) a Joint Permanent Secretary to the Treasury concerned with management and personnel matters throughout all Government departments (Head of the Civil Service); and (c) Head of the Cabinet Secretariat. This last post went to Sir Burke Trend, who was then only forty-eight and is still the present holder of the office.

One issue directly affecting the labours of the Secretariat is the expansion in peace-time of the Cabinet Committee system, since nearly all these committees are serviced by Secretariat personnel. Morrison, in his *Government and Parliament* gives a good account as only an insider can, of the various Cabinet committees established by Prime Minister Attlee between 1945 and 1950. There were committees on defence, civil defence, economic co-ordination, social services, production, legislation, Commonwealth affairs, information, civil aviation, development areas, National Health Service, housing, fuel, etc., etc. Well might Morrison declare, 'The excellent Cabinet Secretariat is a tower of strength.' (Morrison, 1954, 26) It is as vital to the smooth running of any modern Cabinet as oil is to the modern automobile.

5

The Cabinet Office today

The phrase 'Cabinet Secretariat' and 'Cabinet Office' are often employed as though they were synonymous and indeed have been so used in this book. Strictly speaking, however, the Cabinet Office includes both an Historical Section and the Central Statistical Office in addition to the Secretariat proper. The modern tendency is to speak of the 'Cabinet Office' when, in most cases, the 'Secretariat' is intended. This pedantic distinction is of little practical importance but the student should be aware of it. In this chapter the work of these two ancillary sections, History and Statistics, is first described, and then a look is taken at the organization of the Secretariat itself. Finally, there are some speculations on the power exercised behind the scenes by a Secretary to the Cabinet.

The Historical Section

The origin of this small body of full-time and part-time historians can be traced to the Russo-Japanese war of 1902/4. It was decided in 1907 that an impartial review of the events of that war would be a useful exercise for the Committee of Imperial Defence to undertake. The work continued until 1913 and even during the 1914/18 war a staff of four was retained. Since then there has been no shortage of work or source material for the annalist to chronicle. Military operations of the First World War have been comprehensively recorded covering events in East Africa, Macedonia and Mesopotamia, as well as the carnage on the Western Front. Not only battle campaigns have been recorded. The Cabinet Office has also published reports on the hygiene, pathology and surgery of the troops; on the Army's veterinary and transportation services; and on the blockade of Germany and her allies.

The Second World War has been most thoroughly documented by the Historical Section. Amongst its publications are: twenty volumes on the various campaigns, e.g., the War against Japan (five volumes); four treatises on military government, e.g., 'Allied Military Administration in Italy'; a chronological six-volume series on the 'Grand Strategy of the War'; a six-volume 'Popular Military History'; a three-volume 'History of the Royal Air Force' 1939/45; and seventeen volumes on the work of the medical services in the three branches of H.M. Forces.

The publications just referred to are entirely military in character. The 'S.O.E. in France', by M. R. D. Foot, describes the work of both military and civilian agents in the French Underground Movement during the war years and was specially commissioned by the Foreign Office. Finally, there are over twenty volumes in the Civil Series, including such works as 'Problems of Social Policy' by R. M. Titmuss, and 'Economic Blockade' by W. N. Medlicott. As can be deduced from the names of these two authors, the works are written by professional historians, English and Commonwealth, and not normally by members of the Historical Section staff, although its joint Chief Historians, Professor Sir James Butler and Sir Keith Hancock edited respectively the military and civil volumes already mentioned, both officers acting in a part-time capacity. (Sir Keith indeed being unpaid for his services.)

The Central Statistical Office

Before 1939 such statistics as were used by the Government were collated and interpreted by individual departments for their own several purposes. With the coming of war the Government soon recognized the need for the extension and overall co-ordination of statistical services and so a Central Economic Information Service was established as part of the Cabinet Office, although its original domicile was a part of the Scotland Yard building, shared with the Flying Squad. It was staffed by economists and statisticians, mainly recruited from the universities and the Civil Service. In 1941 this Economic Information Service was disbanded and its work divided between the statisticians who formed the embryo of the new institution, the Central Statistical Office, and the economists who became founder-members of the new Economic Section of the Cabinet Secretariat. This Economic Section was, in the words of Lord Bridges, 'charged with presenting a co-ordinated and objective picture of the economy as a whole, and the economic aspects of projected Government policies.' (Bridges, 1964, 91)

When Cripps became Chancellor of the Exchequer shortly after the war, he soon acquired control of the Economic Section. Although nominally it remained part of the Cabinet Office, Cripps initiated the practice of the Economic Section reporting to the Treasury, and in 1953 the reality of this situation was recognized when the Section was officially transferred to the Treasury.

Meanwhile, the Central Statistical Office had remained (and still remains) a semi-autonomous body, although strictly part of the Cabinet Office. It is responsible both for the co-ordination of statistics issued by various Government departments (e.g., the Wholesale Price Index compiled by the Board of Trade, the Index of Weekly Wage Rates published by the Department of Employment and Productivity), and for collating and analyzing its own statistics from material provided by other departments. The Government's Annual Abstract of Statistics, for instance, is a fascinating publication and the student who does not read Statistics should at least glance at a library copy since in no other way can he appreciate the incredible range of topics now covered by Government statistics, from Accidents to Zinc. These topics include—at random— Population, Health, Crime, Education, Wage Rates, Industrial Production and Employment, Highways, and the consumption of beer, to give only a small selection. To deal with these matters, the senior staff of the Central Statistical Office includes a 'Head of the Government Statistical Services' (Professor C. A. Moser), a Deputy Director, an Assistant Director and about twenty-five Statisticians and five Executive Officers. Its annual budget is about £250,000

Partly as a result of a House of Commons Estimates Committee investigation into the Government's statistical services, a fresh look was taken in 1968 into the future role of the Central Statistical Office, and, in consequence, several changes were made. First, new units were established at the C.S.O. to work closely with other relevant Government departments in connexion with the technical aspects of co-ordination, integration and overall planning. Secondly, the C.S.O. became responsible for planning the increased use of computers in the production of all Government statistics (e.g., in the maintenance of time series data banks). Thirdly, the Census Office of the Board of Trade was widened in scope to become a Business Statistics Office responsible for all the main industrial statistics, and the C.S.O. began to supervise the management of this new office. Fourthly, a Research and Special Studies Division was established within the C.S.O., working on such projects as forecasting techniques, measurement of economic growth, etc. Outsiders will be invited to join this Division from time to time on a part-time consultancy basis. Last, more attention is to be given to the dissemination of statistical information by the issuing of new publications, e.g., *Statistical News*, a Quarterly first published in May 1968 (from where, incidentally, much of this information has been culled). Whatever changes in the machinery of our central administration the 1970s may bring, it seems reasonable to forecast that the work of the Central Statistical Office will increase in importance.

The Organization of the Cabinet Secretariat

The Secretariat proper, engaged almost non-stop in the servicing of Cabinet and ministerial committees, has a deservedly high reputation for quiet efficiency. In 1968 its establishment of senior staff was : one Secretary (Salary £9,200 p.a.), three Deputy Secretaries (£6,300 p.a. each), five Under-Secretaries (£5,250 p.a. each), seven Assistant Secretaries (£3,500-£4,000 p.a. each) and eight Principals (£2,335-£3,192 p.a. each). Apart from the Secretary, Sir Burke Trend, these staff members are Administrative Grade civil servants, temporarily seconded from other Government departments. For example, in November 1968 Mr Michael Rose, then the senior of the three Deputy Secretaries, returned to the Foreign Office, his former Department, to be replaced by Sir Robin Hooper also from the Foreign Office.

Membership of the team is considered to be a mark of distinction for the civil servants selected and most of the younger Principals, Assistant and Under-Secretaries chosen are expected to climb high up Whitehall's promotion pyramid when they return to their own departments after this spell of duty, usually of from two to four years duration. In addition to the above mentioned 'managerial' personnel there are about two hundred subordinate staff,

Executive and Clerical Grade workers and typists who carry out the necessary paper and delivery work. Between these two levels there are about a dozen senior civil servants, mostly with specialist qualifications such as Scientific Officers, Economists, Cypher and Telecommunication Superintendents, etc. On the payroll also is Sir Solly Zuckerman (£8,500 p.a.) to advise the Cabinet on scientific policy. To what extent Sir Solly has influenced the Cabinet in its thinking is a matter for conjecture. (The decision to build no more aircraft carriers for example?)

When examining the detailed mechanism whereby the Secretariat gets through its daily volume of paper work, the student should remember that this body serves not only the Cabinet proper but also many Cabinet and ministerial committees. Exactly how many of these committees there are is one of Whitehall's most closely guarded secrets. To the student of public administration, the reasons which are held to justify this concealment are difficult to follow. It is apparently believed by Conservative and Labour Cabinets alike that to provide the electorate with any information concerning even the existence of such committees, let alone their membership or their terms of reference, would be to endanger the sanctity of the principle of collective responsibility.

If an unquestioning respect for constitutional myths is the official justification for this secrecy on Cabinet committees, it sounds rather naïve to any serious student of British politics in the 1960s, if only for the following two reasons: First, no one surely believes that in a world growing increasingly complex, the home-spun politicians who make up the average Cabinet would reach a technical decision, e.g., approving the construction of gas-cooled nuclear reactors, without relying heavily on expert advice. Secondly, in recent years the doctrine of collective responsibility has become noticeably less sacrosanct. For instance, there have been many press reports of disagreements within the Cabinet. Even so responsible a paper as the *Guardian*, on 1 May 1967, published a table unequivocably listing those Cabinet members for and those members against the proposal that Her Majesty's Government apply to join the European Economic Council. The President of the Board of Trade was one member named as opposing the decision to apply and his department was obviously most crucially concerned with the issue. Yet he did not resign until four months later, whilst none of the other reported opponents resigned at all. This is not to suggest that they ought to have resigned. The incident is cited only to support the contention that the principle of collective responsibility is not so inviolable as some political purists would have us believe. Consequently it seems a pity that the doctrine should be used as an excuse for obscuring facts which the student should properly be allowed to learn about Cabinet and Ministerial committees.

Nevertheless, despite official taciturnity the existence of literally dozens of these committees may safely be assumed Here are a few of the Cabinet Committees referred to in the Press in 1968 : Immigration (chaired by the Home Secretary); Legislation; Defence and Overseas Policy; Political and Parliamentary; Co-ordination of Social Services; Economic Affairs and the Home Emergency, though it is doubtful if this last-mentioned Committee has done much since its decision in 1967 to bomb the Torrey Canyon oil tanker. In 1968 a new Political and Parliamentary Committee of the Cabinet was formed, apparently briefed to consider long-term implications of Government policies. Incidentally, the usual practice is for a parallel committee of civil servants to work in conjunction with each Cabinet Committee. Full Cabinet meetings, therefore form a very small part, albeit the most important part, of the overall regular work of the Cabinet Secretariat which normally has several meetings to service every day.

At most of these meetings, including those of the full Cabinet, business is conducted in a relatively informal manner. Motions are not proposed and seconded for instance, nor are votes taken as a general rule. Shorthand writers and tape recorders are viewed with suspicion, and it seems are rarely, if ever used. Nevertheless, many writers with inside knowledge, including Cabinet ministers themselves, have lavishly praised committee secretaries for their professional skill in the rapid and accurate summarizing of decisions taken at Cabinet and Cabinet Committee meetings.

Usually two members of the Secretariat staff are allocated to each committee. The respective ranks of these two civil servants will vary according to the relative importance of the committee they serve but each pair will consist of a senior and junior officer, e.g., an Assistant Secretary and a Principal. This system of joint secretaries has three advantages. First, there is a spare man available if it is found necessary to telephone for a file or individual unexpectedly required. Secondly, there is a reserve to call on in an emergency and in making the summary one can confer with the other on any moot point. Thirdly, the junior gains an invaluable insight into the subtleties of top secretarymanship and into the interplay of departmental hierarchies. Two or three years experience gained as an onlooker at high level discussions between sectional interests can be salutary corrective training for any up-and-coming civil servant otherwise liable to don blinkers soon after returning to his ministerial habitat.

Committee work involves the secretaries in much more than the attending and recording of meetings. A senior Secretary is also responsible for guiding the chairman as to when the meeting should be held and what the agenda should include; for ensuring that all concerned are informed well beforehand; for tactfully prodding committee members if their progress is flagging behind schedule; for ensuring that all necessary papers are obtained, duplicated and circulated in advance to members (the nearer the committee is to the summit—the Cabinet— the more likely it is that papers are required concerning most agenda items); for preparing any reports or material asked for by his committee; for maintaining close contact through the private offices of ministers in charge of those departments directly associated with the committee's work; for ensuring that the committee's discussions do not go beyond its terms of reference in such a way as to overlap with the work of some other committee; and so on.

This danger of overlapping is always present, with so many committees meeting and breeding their own subcommittees. Consequently special attention has to be given to the problems of co-ordination. In the first place, topics covered are grouped into three main divisions—economic affairs, social policy and overseas policy—and each of the three Deputy Secretaries is responsible for one of these categories, charged among other things with ensuring that there is no unnecessary duplication of work arising from the activities of committees within his division. Secondly, a small co-ordinating group is briefed to keep a special watch on those topics which may quite fairly affect more than one of these three broad divisions. The Rhodesia issue for example, clearly must have affected overseas policy as well as economic affairs. Thirdly, members of the Secretariat see the minutes prepared for many committees other than their own, and minutes of each committee meeting are circulated to other interested bodies as well as to the actual committee members.

The amount of paper-work flowing in and out of the Cabinet Office is staggering to contemplate. A typical Cabinet meeting might have about six items on the agenda necessitating about twenty typed foolscap pages per meeting. This is a far cry from the days when Gladstone used to jot his agenda items down on the back of an envelope.

But even so, in terms of quantity it is only the tip of the iceberg. Arising from a case in 1967, where a Cabinet Office typist was convicted under the Official Secrets Act, an official enquiry reported that 13,000 pages of classified documents were prepared every day in the Cabinet Office (about fifty separate papers of just over three pages each with eighty copies of each paper—these figures are all daily averages).

In passing, this case provided a remarkable sidelight on the difficulties of obtaining competent routine shorthand typists in the central London labour market in the late 1960s. Apparently the typist concerned lived in Halifax, went to the local Employment Exchange to enquire about vacancies and was asked by the clerk there if she had thought of going to work in London, because he knew there was a typing and shorthand vacancy in the Cabinet Office in Whitehall. After an interview by the Civil Service Establishment Officer, she was appointed to the Cabinet Office typing pool. Later, although her Superintendent and her seniors expressed dissatisfaction with her work and time-keeping, it was decided not to dismiss her owing to the difficulty of obtaining a replacement 'under the conditions and for the salaries offered'. (H.M.S.O., 1967, 6)

Clearly there has to be a highly efficient organization in constant operation to cope with both the production and distribution of this mass of paper-work. Normal G.P.O. services, even the 5d. first-class variety, could never meet the Secretariat's demand for the safe and speedy despatch of the minutes of the many meetings held each day. There is also, of course, a constant stream of incoming memoranda needed to help prepare agendas of future meetings. Accordingly, a Distribution Section, staffed by Clerical and Executive officers, has been established to concentrate solely on this aspect of the Secretariat's duties. The section operates a twenty-four-hour service, its members working on a shift basis. Papers received from the various committees are sorted into London delivery zones and thrice daily—morning, early afternoon and evening—are delivered in their prominent red boxes by security vans; the area is covered along routes carefully planned from circulation lists, prepared by small groups of officers organized to serve each committee. A committee secretary will have clerical staff allocated to him, and once he has dictated the minutes or summary, and approved the typed draft, it is usually left to the clerk to check its duplication and to place the copies of the minutes, together with any corresponding reports etc., in sealed envelopes. The clerk then attaches the necessary circulation list (previously compiled by the Secretary) and sends the lot to the Distribution Section. It would be most unusual for the minutes not to have been drafted, dictated, duplicated and distributed within twenty-four hours of the meeting concerned.

The normal 'chain of command' pattern, characteristic of most Government departments, is only loosely applied to the Cabinet Secretariat since, by its very nature, the Office is rather different in function from other ministries, and consequently rank becomes less important. For instance, to supervise generally the clerical staff referred to above there are a few Higher Executive Officers, but for most day-to-day purposes the committee clerk works mainly in alliance with 'his' committee secretary. At higher levels, although the committee secretaries themselves are subordinate to the Cabinet Secretary and Deputy Secretaries for general administrative purposes, they collaborate with, and receive orders concerning work on past, present and future meetings, from 'their' committee chairman. Whether enquiring about a future agenda or tactfully chasing a report asked for at an earlier meeting, the committee secretaries are allowed fairly free access to the private offices of the various ministers, with whose personnel they have to deal. In the main, the executive, clerical and typing staff may be regarded as permanent Cabinet Office employees, whilst, as has been said, the administrative officers who serve as secretaries to the various committees, are temporarily seconded from their parent departments. The Cabinet Secretary himself, however, once appointed, holds office until retirement day, and his post is rightly regarded with great respect within and beyond Whitehall. He is, after all, one of the three leading civil servants in the land, receiving the same salary as the Permanent Secretaries to the Treasury and to the Civil Service Department, i.e. £9,200 p.a. which is £600 p.a. above that of the Permanent Secretaries in other departments. Finally, in comparison with other Ministries such as Agriculture or Transport, the staff is small in number, highly geared as regards the ratio of administrative to routine officers, and nearly all of them are housed under one roof. This means that, as with many self-contained organizations, staff members soon come to know and understand each other and consequently to work well together towards a common end. There is no occasion for intersection rivalry such as is often found inside large departments and, indeed, such rivalry rarely exists within the Cabinet Office circles.

The Power of the Cabinet Secretariat

Such an aura of secrecy surrounds the Cabinet Office that an outsider can only speculate on the degree of influence exercised by the Cabinet Secretary and others behind the scenes.

First, however, a distinction should be made between the Cabinet Office in Whitehall and the Prime Minister's Private Office at No. 10 Downing Street, both of which are staffed by civil servants. The division of responsibility between these two is fairly clear in theory, but in practice may sometimes become blurred. The Prime Minister's

Private Office, 'the No. 10 network' as it is sometimes suspiciously referred to, is responsible for serving the Prime Minister's personal needs in such matters as his engagement diary and daily time-table, his constituency affairs, Honours List recommendations for submission to the Queen, his relations with Press and B.B.C., and links with his Party rank and file. The busiest of Premiers forgets at his peril the daily chat with his linkman, the party's Chief Whip. A Conservative Prime Minister may be better served by his Central Party Office as regards public relations than is his Labour counterpart by Transport House. Hence Mr Wilson's attempts to remedy this shortcoming by the establishment in 1964 of a political section at No. 10, charged with securing the maximum harmony possible between Cabinet and the Parliamentary Party.

Mr Wilson once declared that it was his intention to make No. 10 'a power-house, not a monastery'. This phrase can mean different things to different people. Ian Trethowan, for instance, writing in *The Times* on 6 June 1968, felt that the term 'No. 10' was 'clearly intended to mean not just the Prime Minister's personal entourage but the Cabinet Office, which spreads round the corner into Whitehall'. The Prime Minister chooses his own senior staff for No. 10, perhaps introducing as his Private Secretary someone who had previously served him in a similar role, as Macmillan was served by John Wyndham in the Treasury and the Foreign Office before they both arrived at No. 10. Mr Wilson has said that he favours people with 'earthy' experiences, e.g., promising civil servants from the Ministries such as Agriculture and Power as well as budding diplomats from the Foreign Office. Hand-picked private secretaries of top calibre may quite properly exert some influence over the Prime Minister's thinking. What is important is that they should not be 'yes-men'. Lloyd George once reminded Winston Churchill during the latter's wartime Premiership, how important it was for a Prime

Minister to be surrounded by people who would stand up to him and say 'No, No, No', This is surely true. No small part of Mr Macmillan's success as a Prime Minister was the candid advice he could always expect from such Private Secretaries as Timothy Bligh and John Wyndham.

The fact that the Prime Minister's personal staff is so small in number contrasted with, say, that of the American President, only makes it more likely that these confidantes, being so few, have greater opportunities than most 'inner circle' men of counselling the Prime Minister. But an outsider cannot assess the weight of such influence separately from that of the key men in the Cabinet Office. It is indeed rather symbolic that the Cabinet Office quarters and No. 10 are structurally linked by a web of underground corridors. Continuing to take Macmillan as an example, Norman Brook had probably as much influence with him as anyone else, for example in such tasks as the preparation of Macmillan's famous 'Winds of Change' speech delivered in Cape Town in 1959.

Sometimes an attempt is made to distinguish between the Prime Minister's Office and the Cabinet Office by claiming that the former exists solely to serve the Prime Minister, while the latter's function is to serve the whole Cabinet. But this seems to be a distinction of doubtful validity, reminding us of Asquith's famous observation that the office of Prime Minister is what the holder makes of it. Mr Wilson for one had no doubt what he considered to be the position. When asked in a radio interview in 1964 'But it [The Cabinet Office] would be totally under your command, rather than under the command of the Cabinet?' Mr Wilson, not then Prime Minister, replied without hesitation, 'The Cabinet Secretariat has never been under the control of the Cabinet.' (B.B.C., 1964, 28)

Speaking on the B.B.C. Third Programme in 1967, after two and a half years experience at No. 10, Mr Wilson explained the dual role of the Cabinet Office as follows:

In the first place the Cabinet Office exists partly to service the Cabinet and Cabinet committees, to provide accurate records of discussion so that a Cabinet decision is a decision understood by all departments and not just an account of a discussion; and so that papers are prepared adequately, Ministers fully briefed and issues brought to a clear point of decision. But, in addition, the Cabinet Secretariat is the private department of the Prime Minister. Each member of the Cabinet Office staff services and serves the whole Cabinet but they are also my own staff. If you take for example, the Permanent Secretary of the Cabinet—he is the servant of the whole Cabinet and attends all its meetings; but he is also my Permanent Secretary in the same sense that any other Minister has a Permanent Secretary/Chief Adviser. He advises me, briefs me, not only for Cabinet meetings and other Cabinet committees over which I preside, but on the general running of the government so far as policy is concerned (B.B.C., 6 April 1967, 447)

It is not unreasonable to argue that a Prime Minister is entitled to specialist professional advice as much as is any departmental minister. By the same token ministers without portfolio should have equal access to the counselling services of No. 10. But it is questionable if they do. Nowhere in that same lengthy interview did the Prime Minister give any indication that such was the case.

Everyone realizes that in an age growing increasingly complex, the man at the top in any large-scale organization must rely to a large extent on papers prepared and counsels given by his close advisers. The important thing is, of course, that these advisers should be men of sound judgment and, in the case of the Cabinet Secretary, of political awareness also. It is this last quality which some Cabinet Secretaries may have lacked. Take, for instance, Hankey's assurance to Neville Chamberlain after the Munich settlement of 1938: 'At every point your touch was unerring, your vision prophetic' (Feiling, 1946, 379)—

a view less brutal than Lloyd George's famous comment on Chamberlain: 'A good Lord Mayor of Birmingham in an off year', but perhaps no more accurate. Another example—one of the few occasions when the Secretary of the Cabinet received front-page treatment from the national press—arose from Lord Denning's 1963 Report into the Stephen Ward affair. The then Cabinet Secretary, Sir Norman Brook, acting on information received from M.I.5, decided to visit Mr Profumo, Secretary of State for War, in August 1961, to warn him of the potential security risks arising from association with Ward and a Russian Embassy official, Ivanov. But when two years afterwards the House was debating the resignation of the War Minister, as a result of circumstances arising from his friendship with Ward, Prime Minister Macmillan told the House that until February 1963, he had never heard of Mr Ward. Later in the same speech, he said: 'I must tell the House that Sir Norman Brook did not inform me either of the fact that he had received this information from the head of the security service, or that he had thought it his duty to speak a warning word about Mr Ward's friendship with Ivanov. He did not tell me.' (H.C. Debates 17 June 1963) It is impossible not to have some sympathy with Mr Macmillan on this score.

The Future of the Cabinet Office

The 1970s may see an increase in the power of the Cabinet Office within the Civil Service itself. Following a recommendation by the Fulton Committee, the Prime Minister announced in October 1968 the establishment of a new Government department to take over those aspects of Civil Service control and management which had until then been exercised by the Treasury. Although Lord Shackleton was appointed in charge of the Department it was officially stated that the overall head was to be the Prime Minister himself. In the past no senior Civil Servant appointment has been made without the approval of the Treasury. Government 'by the lifted eyebrow' will always be with us but in future it may be the eyebrows of the Secretariat top brass rather than those of the Treasury mandarins which influence the careers of promising high flyers in the Service.

From the earliest peace-time days of the Cabinet Secretariat in the 1920s, there has been intermittent pressure from some Treasury officials to have the Cabinet Office brought within their domain. The office is still officially listed in the annual Estimates as a 'Subordinate Department' of the Treasury. Furthermore, as has been said, for many years Sir Edward Bridges performed the dual role of Permanent Secretary to the Treasury and the Secretary to the Cabinet. Even when he retired in 1953, the link was still maintained in that Sir Norman Brook became Secretary to the Cabinet and also Joint Permanent Secretary at the Treasury, although his duties in this latter post were restricted to establishment work as befits the 'Head of the Civil Service' (his supplementary official title). From now on, however, whilst the Treasury will continue to be a most powerful department, the Cabinet Office for all practical purposes will operate more than ever as a completely independent unit.

Conclusion

In short, Cabinet Secretaries have always had opportunities to influence Prime Ministers and there is no doubt that they have, quite properly, made use of these opportunities on occasions. It would indeed place any Prime Minister at a disadvantage not to have, as do most of his ministers, a respected and trusted Permanent Secretary in whom he can confide and from whom he can seek advice. This advice will have two merits additional to those derived from the intrinsic qualities of the counsellor. First, it comes from an officer who may have experienced life under several Prime Ministers—Brooks, for instance, served under Attlee, Churchill, Eden and Macmillan; secondly, the counsel is likely to be free from any departmental bias, whereas the advice any Prime Minister receives from his Cabinet colleagues may not be so impartial or unprejudiced.

How sound has been the advice proffered in the past can only be a matter of conjecture. There is little doubt, however, that Prime Ministers themselves have made bad policy decisions despite, and not because of the courses urged upon them by their Cabinet Secretaries. What seems wrong to the student of public administration is not that the advice given may sometimes be faulty—only a fool would expect his advisers to be right on every issue—but that an atmosphere of mystery should surround the functions and organization of the Cabinet Office. Of course, the advice given by Officials to the Queen's chief minister must be treated as confidential. There may be a case—though it is less obvious—for the red-taped curtain drawn over the membership, activities, and even the existence of Cabinet committees. But there seems no case at all for arguing that the confidential nature of the job at its highest levels must preclude the student from learning about both the routine organization of work among the lower echelons or the machinery which exists for decision making within Cabinet circles.

Take for example Mr Wilson's public insistence that he is kept well informed on all major issues involving any of his ministries. Exactly how does he acquire this knowledge? Do the Cabinet Office staff prepare their briefs from papers supplied to them by the departments concerned? If so, might not the minister or his departmental head divulge only such information as he considers expedient? If, on the other hand, the Cabinet Office staff maintain

independent records in order to be able to give the Prime
Minister whatever data he requires concerning an issue
such as output of North Sea gas, or communistic influence
within a trade union, must not a disturbing amount of
duplication of records be incurred? Perhaps a part of
the process of keeping a Prime Minister informed involves
his having men on various inter-departmental committees
who are authorized to report to him directly. But if so,
must not this arrangement cut across the normal chain
of command? These queries are not quibbles. Clearly there
is an administrative problem here, in essence one not
peculiar to Whitehall but common to all pyramid patterns
of management structure. How the boss can delegate, yet
retain control and remain aware is one of the oldest questions in the management game, and it would be of practical
value to learn how the question is answered inside the
Cabinet Office.

Has not the taxpayer who finds the million pounds
needed each year to keep the Cabinet Office in business a
right to such information? To use a phrase of one of Mr
Wilson's own Cabinet Ministers, we are 'entitled to know'
of these things. The science of public administration will
become increasingly important in the 1970s. That potential
administrators should be denied the chance to examine
the methods and techniques used by the Cabinet Office
in its daily processing of data and servicing of committees
is less than fair. It is in the hope that others may be en-
couraged to chisel away at the ice that this small book has
been written.

Appendix A
The Commonwealth Secretariat

Before the mid-sixties, the Cabinet Secretariat worked with the Commonwealth Relations Office in the servicing of the numerous Commonwealth conferences, especially those of Prime Ministers which were held at irregular intervals in London. Servicing in this sense also included much hospitality work as well as the organizing and recording of business sessions. This arrangement, despite its many practical advantages, grew increasingly irksome, particularly to some of the newer partners in the Commonwealth because it seemed to imply a relationship—the Mother Country first and the other partners joint-second which was contrary to the whole spirit of an association of members 'equal in status and in no way subordinate one to another'.

At the 1964 London Conference of Commonwealth Prime Ministers there was pressure from such members as Kenya, Ghana, Trinidad, etc., for a Commonwealth Secretariat to be established. This was to be staffed by officials chosen from various Commonwealth countries, not only by British civil servants, and charged with the responsibility for arranging and servicing future Commonwealth Conferences. The pressure was effective and in

January 1965 a meeting of Commonwealth officials was held in London under the chairmanship of Sir Burke Trend, to submit proposals for the establishment of such a Secretariat. This meeting produced a report agreed to by all members and the Secretariat came into being in August 1965 with the appointment of Mr Arnold Smith, a Canadian ex-diplomat, as Secretary General to head a Secretariat with offices in Marlborough House, London. The cost of this Secretariat was to be shared among Commonwealth countries, e.g., The United Kingdom was to meet 30% of the expense, Canada 21%, India 11%, Australia 10%, Uganda 1·5%, etc. (The first annual budget was for £175,000.) In March 1966, the British Parliament passed a Commonwealth Secretariat Act, granting to Secretariat staff diplomatic immunity (including car-parking facilities!) similar to that enjoyed by the staffs of most Embassy and High Commissioner offices in London. The Act also bestowed on the Secretariat a legal personality. It could now sue and be sued in its own name.

When establishing the Secretariat, the Commonwealth Governments wisely refrained from limiting too precisely its power and functions. To quote the Commonwealth Secretary-General in his 1966 Report: 'The Secretariat was set up to discharge tasks which Heads of Government might from time to time assign to it and was left to evolve pragmatically in the light of experience and of their wishes.' Nevertheless, the Commonwealth Prime Ministers in their Agreed Memorandum announcing the establishment of the Secretariat did indicate certain 'guide lines' as to the kind of activity they expected the Secretariat to undertake. (Incidentally, the Secretary-General was to have access to Heads of Government in the same way that the British Cabinet Secretary has direct communication with the British Prime Minister.) Amongst the duties of the Commonwealth Secretariat indicated by the Heads of Government were:

1 To act as an agency for promoting a fuller exchange of views on matters of major international importance.

2 To arrange occasional meetings of officials of member Governments for the exchange of information and views on agreed subjects.

3 To prepare and circulate papers on international questions of common concern to all Commonwealth Governments where it is considered useful to do so.

4 To prepare and circulate 'balanced' papers on the constitutional advance of the remaining dependent territories within the Commonwealth.

5 To 'initiate, collate and distribute' to member Governments reports on economic and social problems, e.g., the inter-relationship of agricultural and industrial growth in the new Commonwealth. The Secretary-General may commission outside experts on a consultancy basis to help him in this work.

6 To keep in touch with 'the various United Nations' agencies whose work in the Commonwealth countries will on occasion be of direct concern to it.'

7 To assist member Governments at their request, who wish to receive support for Development projects within their own communities.

8 To circulate papers on international questions prepared by a member Government if requested to do so by this Government. However, the Secretary-General will have a discretionary power to veto such a request if he considers that the paper concerned 'propagates any sectional or partisan point of view or would for any other reason be liable to be offensive to any member country or countries.'

9 To service meetings of Commonwealth ministers and officials although in this connexion the Secretariat will be able to call in the host country for secretariat assistance as well as help in the arrangements for accommodation, transport, etc.

As regards the meetings of Prime Ministers, the Secretary-General will act as Secretary for each meeting and will also attend to the 'preparation, collation and circulation of papers on agenda items, together with such background papers as appear appropriate; the production of minutes and, with the assistance of the host government, the general organization of the Meeting.'

The Prime Ministers themselves will prepare the actual agenda in the form of a list of broad headings though clearly the Secretary-General may play a useful role here in obtaining common agreement on the contents of the agenda and the order in which agenda items will be discussed.

10 To undertake a 'comprehensive review' of existing intra-Commonwealth organizations to see whether some of them at least could be usefully taken over by the Secretariat.

The Secretariat set to work on this last item and a Review Committee, chaired by Lord Sherfield, an ex-British Ambassador in Washington, met in London in December 1965. The Committee included seven other members, each nominated by a different Commonwealth Government or group of Governments (e.g. Uganda, Kenya and Tanzania jointly chose one representative; as did Jamaica, Trinidad and Tobago) and the Secretary-General himself also took part in the discussions. Ten Commonwealth organizations were considered in detail, viz: Liaison, Economic, Education, Scientific and Forestry Committees; the Institute, the Agricultural Bureaux, the Aeronautical Research Council, the Telecommunications Board and the Air Transport Council.

In August 1966, the Committee completed its review and published its proposals. These included a recommendation that the Economic and Education Committees be integrated with the Secretariat and this has since been implemented. The remaining organizations have been generally left alone, although the Secretary-General has become an ex-officio member of the Forestry Committee. The extension of the Secretariat's activities has led to an increase in its staff. At the end of 1968 its Marlborough House staff numbered about 170, grouped into four main divisions, viz: International and Conference, Economic, Education and Administration. Each division has about four senior staff (equivalent to Principal level or above) recruited on as wide a geographical basis as possible, e.g., there are two Deputy Secretaries-General, one from Ghana and the other from Ceylon.

Perhaps the best way of conveying some impression of the range of activities involving the Commonwealth Secretariat is to list some of the Commonwealth events which the Secretariat serviced during 1968. These included: Educational Conference in Lagos; Nigerian Peace Talks held in Kampala; Medical Conference, also in Kampala; Conference on Teaching of Mathematics in Schools, in Trinidad; and a Meeting of Finance Ministers in London (preceded by a Meeting of Finance Officials). To take just one of these events—the Kampala Medical Conference held from 2 to 12 September—there were 51 papers circulated to all members prior to the Conference, whilst the Official Report of the proceedings contains over 170 pages.

Although conferences of this type do not receive anything like the publicity that the world press showers on Prime Ministers Conferences such as the one held in London in January 1969, a moment's reflection must convince any student of their great worth and of the value of a Commonwealth Secretariat which enables the necessary administrative machinery to run smoothly and efficiently.

Contemporary events in Rhodesia and Nigeria have formed a tragic background to the early years of the Commonwealth Secretariat. Despite such handicaps the Secretariat has been able to quietly to establish and consolidate itself and it now enjoys a deserved reputation as an organization which is doing much to promote Commonwealth harmony.

Appendix B
Careers of the Cabinet Secretaries

1916-1938   Maurice Pascal Alers Hankey, born 1877. Education: Rugby and Royal Naval College, Greenwich. 1899: Captain in Royal Marine Artillery. 1902: Seconded to Naval Intelligence. 1908: Assistant Secretary, Committee of Imperial Defence. 1912: Secretary, Committee of Imperial Defence. 1914: Secretary to War Council. 1916: Secretary to War Cabinet. 1923: Clerk to Privy Council. 1938: On retirement, became Lord Hankey.

1938-1947   Edward Bridges, born 1892, son of the Poet Laureate, Robert Bridges. Educated at Eton and Magdalen. 1914/18: Army Officer, Awarded M.C. 1919: Entered Treasury. 1938: Secretary to Cabinet: 1945: Permanent Secretary to Treasury, whilst still remaining as Cabinet Secretary. (In order to help share this work-load, Norman Brook was appointed as additional Cabinet Secretary.) 1947: Retired as Cabinet Secretary. 1956: Retired as Secretary to the Treasury. Became Lord Bridges.

1947-1962   Norman Brook, born 1902. Educated at Wolverhampton School and Wadham College, Oxford. 1925/1938: Home Office—several appointments in various sections, finally Assistant Secretary in Charge of civil emergencies and Defence Regulations. 1938/1942: Private Secretary to Sir John Anderson. 1942: Deputy Secretary of the Cabinet. 1943: Permanent Secretary to Minister of Reconstruction. 1945: Joint Secretary to the Cabinet. 1947: Secretary to the Cabinet. 1956: Joint Permanent Secretary at Treasury, whilst retaining post as Cabinet Secretary. 1962: Retired from Civil Service. Became Lord Normanbrook.

1963 to Present: Burke St John Trend, born 1914. Educated at Whitgift School, and Merton College, Oxford. 1936: Board of Education. 1937: Treasury. 1939: Assistant Private Secretary to Chancellor of Exchequer. 1945: Principal Private Secretary to the Chancellor of the Exchequer. 1949: Under-Secretary —Treasury. 1956: Deputy Secretary to Cabinet. 1959: Third Secretary—Treasury. 1960: Second Secretary —Treasury, assisting Sir Norman Brook. 1963: Secretary of the Cabinet.

Suggestions for further reading

So far as is known, no previous book dealing solely with the British Cabinet office has been published. Of the books listed in the Bibliography perhaps the most useful on this topic are the two books by Lord Hankey; 'Records of the Cabinet Office to 1922' published by the H.M.S.O.; Daalder's *Cabinet Reform*; and the general survey by Chester and Willson.

Other standard works containing helpful references include:

JENNINGS, SIR IVOR, *Cabinet Government*, 1959, Cambridge U.P.
MACKENZIE, W. J. M. and GROVE, J. W., *Central Administration in Britain*, 1957, Longmans.
MACKINTOSH, J., *The British Cabinet*, 1962, Stevens.

Of articles written about the Cabinet Office by far the most informative is: Hewison, R., 'The Organization of the Cabinet Secretariat', *O and M Bulletin*, (December 1951).

Other articles which can be recommended are:

TRETHOWAN, I., 'A Look at Mr Wilson's Power-House', *The Times*, (6 June 1968).
HUNT, N., 'The Prime Minister and the Machinery of Government', *The Listener* (6 April 1967).
BRANDON, H. and NEUSTADT, R. E., '10 Downing Street—Is it out of date?', *Sunday Times* (8 November 1964).

Now only of historical interest are:

STARR, J. R., 'The English Cabinet Secretariat', *American Political Science Review* (May 1928).

JONES, C., 'The War Cabinet Secretariat', *Empire Review* (December 1923. January 1924).

CRAICK, H., 'The Cabinet Secretariat', *Nineteenth century* (June 1922).

For the reader who can manage to visit London, Cabinet conclusions and papers can be studied at the Public Record Office in Chancery Lane. (No previous notice of an intended visit is necessary.) Unfortunately records of Cabinet proceedings within the last thirty years are not available to the public.

Bibliography

BASSETT, R., *Nineteen Thirty One*, (1958), Macmillan.
B.B.C. PUBLICATIONS, *Whitehall and Beyond*, (1964).
BEAVERBROOK, LORD, *Men and Power*, (1956), Hutchinson.
BRIDGES, LORD, *The Treasury*, (1964), Allen and Unwin.
CHESTER, D. N. and WILLSON, F. M. G., *The Organisation of British Central Government 1914-1956*, (1957), Allen and Unwin.
CHURCHILL, SIR WINSTON, *The Second World War*, (1949), Volume 2, Cassell.
—*The Second World War*, (1950), Volume 3, Cassell.
—*The Second World War*, (1951), Volume 4, Cassell.
—*The Second World War*, (1952), Volume 5, Cassell.
DAALDER, H., *Cabinet Reform in Britain 1914-1963*, (1964), Oxford U.P.
EHRMAN, J., *Cabinet Government and War*, (1958), Cambridge U.P.
FEILING, SIR KEITH, *The Life of Neville Chamberlain*, (1946), Macmillan.
HANKEY, LORD, *Diplomacy by Conference*, (1946), Ernest Benn.
—*The Supreme Command*, (1961), Allen and Unwin.
H.M.S.O., Records of the Cabinet Office to 1922, (1966).
—Report of the Security Commission, (1967), Cmnd 3365.
ISMAY, LORD, *Memoirs of Lord Ismay*, (1960), Heinemann.
JOHNSON, F. A., *Defence by Committee*, (1960), Oxford U.P.
MORRISON OF LAMBETH, LORD, *Government and Parliament*, (1954), Oxford U.P.
—*An Autobiography*, (1960), Odham.

BIBLIOGRAPHY

NICHOLSON, SIR HAROLD, *King George V: His Life and Reign*, (1952), Constable.

SOMERVELL, D. C., *The Reign of King George the Fifth*, (1935), Faber and Faber.

TAYLOR, A. J. P., *English History 1914-1945*, (1965), Oxford U.P.

VANSITTART, LORD, *The Mist Procession*, (1958), Hutchinson.